MW00610077

With a close reading of maj(
engages in deep and creative theological reflection on their contributions to
contemporary life. He draws upon a lifetime of experience as both teacher
and minister to address complex theological and ethical issues clearly and
concisely, thus inviting readers to share in the adventure of biblical study
that is enriching and transformative. This book offers an important correc-
tive for all those who think of the Old Testament as merely "old" and
irrelevant for the life of faith. The "life lessons" Tuck discerns in the biblical
portraits of Moses, Jeremiah, Esther, Ruth, and a host of other exemplary
characters deserve and reward thoughtful attention.

—Samuel E. Balentine, DPhil
Professor of Old Testament, Emeritus
Union Presbyterian Seminary
Richmond, Virginia

In *Lessons from Old Testament Characters*, Dr. William Powell Tuck has
compiled a volume that is both confessionally and academically important.
In these sixteen sermons, which he has earlier delivered, he demonstrates
his skill both in the pulpit and as a teacher well-grounded academically.
The typical churchman will find important materials about the meaningful
living of one's life, and the individual wishing to understand the academic
undergirding of the material will also find data about the literary-historical
nature of the text. Typical of the development is a sentence in chapter 1,
"Adam and Eve: Our Story," where he states, "It is difficult to comprehend
how anyone reading it cannot see clearly its poetical, parabolic, allegorical,
and mythical depiction . . . ."

The book is one from which an individual will profit, but it would also
be an excellent volume for a study guide as a class or study group seeks to
understand and appreciate this ancient text within our modern setting.

—Frank E. Eakin Jr., PhD
Former Weinstein-Rosenthal Professor of Jewish and Christian Studies
Department of Religious Studies
University of Richmond, Virginia

In *Lessons from Old Testament Characters*, William Powell Tuck considers both well-known and lesser-known men and women of the Old Testament with a view toward their lived faith. With Tuck's help, one quickly realizes that these heroes are not dead and gone with nothing to offer readers in the twenty-first century. Instead, while our world and theirs are different in many ways, faithful living remains a challenge and the Old Testament remains a source of inspiration.

In fact, it is helpful to realize that even these biblical characters stumbled at times. Adam and Eve disobeyed and cast blame; Abraham put his own safety ahead of Sarah's; Jacob schemed; Esau was impulsive; David committed adultery; Elijah and Jeremiah despaired; Naaman wanted fireworks. As to our humanity, we are not worlds away after all.

Yet there is more, for these characters and others like them found a better way through community, forgiveness, blessing, self-control, love, acceptance, courage, and faith. Even more so, these stories testify not only to human resilience but also to the enduring presence of God and to how God renews life both in ordinary and extraordinary ways.

When it comes to living faithfully amid the struggle, we have much to consider by way of *Lessons from Old Testament Characters*. Bill Tuck delivers these lessons with sermonic clarity, well-seasoned theology, and pastoral insight. There are many other biblical characters to consider; one can hope, therefore, that another volume in is the works.

—Warren C. Robertson, PhD
Associate Professor of Biblical Studies
Gardner-Webb University, School of Theology

William Powell Tuck's *Lessons from Old Testament Characters* puts the Bible first. He has studied the biblical text in the company of biblical scholars and theologians, and he retells these Old Testament stories with a sure sense of what is relevant and needful for Christians. Tuck does not use his chosen characters simply to illustrate commonly held understandings and values. Decades of careful study and pastoral experience bear fruit in challenging theological reflection and refreshing practical applications.

—Pamela J. Scalise, PhD
Senior Professor of Old Testament
Fuller Theological Seminary.

LESSONS FROM OLD TESTAMENT CHARACTERS

Smyth & Helwys Publishing, Inc.
6316 Peake Road
Macon, Georgia 31210-3960
1-800-747-3016
©2021 by William Powell Tuck
All rights reserved.

Library of Congress Cataloging-in-Publication Data

Names: Tuck, William Powell, 1934- author.
Title: Lessons from Old Testament characters / by William Powell Tuck.
Description: First edition. | Macon, GA : Smyth & Helwys Publishing, 2021.
| Includes bibliographical references.
Identifiers: LCCN 2021048034 | ISBN 9781641733403 (paperback)
Subjects: LCSH: Bible. Old Testament--Biography.
Classification: LCC BS571 .T825 2021 | DDC 221.9/22--dc23/eng/20211006
LC record available at https://lccn.loc.gov/2021048034

LESSONS
FROM
OLD
TESTAMENT
CHARACTERS

WILLIAM
POWELL
TUCK

Also by *William Powell Tuck*

Facing Grief and Death

The Struggle for Meaning (editor)

Knowing God: Religious Knowledge in the Theology of John Baillie

Our Baptist Tradition

Ministry: An Ecumenical Challenge (editor)

Getting Past the Pain

A Glorious Vision

The Bible as Our Guide for Spiritual Growth (editor)

Authentic Evangelism

The Lord's Prayer Today

The Way for All Seasons

Through the Eyes of a Child

Christmas Is for the Young… Whatever Their Age

Love as a Way of Living

The Compelling Faces of Jesus

The Left Behind Fantasy

The Ten Commandments: Their Meaning Today

Facing Life's Ups and Downs

The Church in Today's World

The Church Under the Cross

Modern Shapers of Baptist Thought in America

The Journey to the Undiscovered Country: What's Beyond Death?

A Pastor Preaching: Toward a Theology of the Proclaimed Word

The Pulpit Ministry of the Pastors of River Road Church, Baptist
(editor)

The Last Words from the Cross

Lord, I Keep Getting a Busy Signal: Reaching for a Better Spiritual Connection

Overcoming Sermon Block: The Preacher's Workshop

A Revolutionary Gospel: Salvation in the Theology of Walter Rauschenbusch

Holidays, Holy Days, and Special Days

A Positive Word for Christian Lamenting: Funeral Homilies

The Forgotten Beatitude: Worshiping through Stewardship

Star Thrower: A Pastor's Handbook

A Pastoral Prophet: Sermons and Prayers of Wayne E. Oates (editor)

The Abiding Presence: Communion Meditations

Which Voice Will You Follow?

The Difficult Sayings of Jesus

Beginning and Ending a Pastorate

Conversations with My Grandchildren about God, Religion, and Life

Markers Along the Way: The Signs of Jesus in the Gospel of John

The Rebirth of the Church

Jesus' Journey to the Cross

For
Catherine and John;
J. T., Michael, and Emily;
Bill, Angela,
Campbell, and Alden,
who have enriched my life
with their love and support

Contents

Preface

Many find the Old Testament difficult to comprehend with its ancient culture, bizarre rituals and customs, strange stories, primitive concepts of God, and sometimes conflicting views of historical accounts. They often do not see how it can address our modern world with any meaningful religious or cultural insights. So they seldom read it unless they are "forced" to examine it in a Sunday school, college, or seminary class. Preachers may ignore much of it in their preaching because their critical biblical studies have raised many questions in their minds. Several years ago, a book by Donald E. Gowan, *Reclaiming the Old Testament for the Christian Pulpit*, awakened me to the possibility of seeing how genuine modern biblical criticism in my study of the Old Testament could make this early tradition and ancient faith more meaningful for today's world.

This led me to preach a series of sermons on "Heroes of the Old Testament," including individual sermons that focused occasionally on one of the Old Testament characters. I also did more detailed Bible studies on Wednesday nights and some week-long series on a more in-depth study of a biblical character or book, like Jeremiah, Job, Hosea, or Jonah. During these studies, I went into a more careful examination of these books, but I also recognized that more people attend church on Sunday, and I needed to address them through sermons on Old Testament characters at that time.

The sermons in this book represent some of the ones I preached on Old Testament characters in several churches where I served as pastor or interim pastor. I am keenly aware that many noted Old Testament figures like Saul, Samuel, Miriam, Job, Micah, Amos, Hosea, Jonah, and others are not included in this volume. Maybe that will call for an additional work later. I trust that this book will be helpful for ministers and laypeople alike as they strive to understand the Old Testament writings better. I have found that the Old Testament is a superb resource for personal study, for spiritual enrichment, and for preaching. I send this volume out with the hope that others will likewise be inspired to study, teach, and preach this sacred testament.

I express my appreciation to Rand Forder, a fellow minister, for his careful proofreading of my manuscript. He has been a faithful resource in helping me avoid mindless mistakes. I am indebted also to Frank Eakin Jr., former Weinstein-Rosenthal Professor of Jewish and Christian Studies, Department of Religious Studies at the University of Richmond, Virginia, who read my manuscript and offered valuable suggestions that enabled me to improve and clarify my thoughts.

Adam and Eve: Our Story

Genesis 2:4-24; 3:1-22

The Genesis story about Adam and Eve is one of the oldest stories we have recorded. It is a timeless tale that captures our attention even in our modern, scientific world. Some have dismissed it because they reject the literalism ascribed to it by ultra-fundamentalist voices. It is difficult to comprehend how anyone reading it cannot see clearly its poetical, parabolic, allegorical, and mythical depiction in a garden where God is described as walking and talking to Adam and Eve and needs to rest after six days of creating, where a serpent speaks and there are flaming swords and magic trees. In "poetic" language, not a historical proclamation, and in anthropological imagery, the ancient writer is seeking to project the wonder of God's creation with the crowning focus on the creation of humanity.

This Genesis account, sometimes called the "pearl of Genesis," is not meant to be understood as a scientific or verbatim rendering of creation, but as an affirmation about God as Creator. Michelangelo's painting in the Sistine Chapel has drawn people through the years to focus on this ancient story. The virtually unknown writings of Mark Twain, "Extracts from Adam's Diary," "Eve's Diary," and the "Autobiography of Eve," were drawn from this epic story, as was Ernest Hemingway's posthumously published novel *The Garden of Eden*. Books such as Bill Moyers's *Genesis: A Living Conversation*, based on his public television series several years ago, and the recently published book *The First Love Story: Adam, Eve, and Us* by Bruce Feiler (2017) have reminded us of the continuing freshness, excitement, and inspiration sparked by this first story about the beginning of humanity. Bestselling author Dan Brown published *Origin* in 2018; the novel wrestles with the continuing question, "Where do we come from and where are we going?"

Allegorical Interpretation

Maybe the writer of Genesis is speaking like Shakespeare, who described the forest of Arden as having "tongues in trees, books in the running brooks, sermons in stones, and good in everything."[1] The literal-minded person would say that this is nonsense. Through symbolic words, Shakespeare conveyed insights that are not factually true. No one would argue that the parables of Jesus must be taken as historical narratives in order to understand the message Jesus was trying to express through them. When he said, "I am the light of the world," "I am the door," "I am the vine," or "I am the good shepherd," Jesus was speaking metaphorically. The story of the prodigal son may have been the story of a particular man. However, it is probably not a historical account but a parable of Everyman. The parable calls us to look into the mirror and see ourselves.

Parables and allegories are not limited by science or age but are ageless in the message they seek to bear. God inspires men and women, not books, and is present in the written words because God was in the minds and hearts of the writers. The written words, then, become a witness to the revelation. The words that are used are symbolic and may vary in meaning according to the cultural milieu and experience of humanity. Hence the words must be interpreted and reinterpreted to have meaning for each age. God is Creator and Redeemer whether the world is conceived scientifically as flat, square, or round. It is not necessary to accept the cosmology of the Genesis writers or understand the story literally in order to acknowledge God as Lord and Creator.

Two Accounts of Creation

It is my understanding that there are at least two accounts of creation in the first two chapters of Genesis. They use a different style and language, and there is a variation in the order of events. One creation story is found in Genesis 1:1–2:4a. This account shows an orderly progression of creation and reflects a high concept of God: God created the heavens, earth, humankind, and the Sabbath by his mighty word. The other story is recorded in Genesis 2:4b-25. This account is much simpler and more primitive than the other. It is much more vivid and anthropomorphic, for it depicts God as breathing, planting, building, and molding. In Genesis 1:1–2:4a, creation follows a design that begins with light and concludes with the creation of humankind. The story in the second chapter of Genesis begins with the creation of man and ends with the creation of woman. But these variations in sequence do not mean that the accounts are irreconcilable. It seems to me that each account makes a unique contribution, that each expresses one facet of the creation faith of Israel. The two accounts seem to be an attempt to give a fuller explanation of one central fact: God is Creator. They are not in conflict with each other but complement each other and enrich one central truth.

That is the significant thing about seeing God in these two creation accounts. God is depicted as sovereign Lord in both. God made the world and humankind, and God will have dominion over all of God's creation. The Genesis accounts can never grow old. They are independent of a day or an hour because they were written for all ages. By expressing the creation accounts in parabolic and mythological form, the writers have not limited the stories to the scientific view of any age. These accounts were probably transmitted orally from generation to generation before they were written down. When the writers finally recorded them as we have them today, the inspiration that guided the authors did not impress them with the scientific conceptions of the twentieth century. Modern science would have had no meaning to the people of that age. But the writers used the worldview of their own day to convey a truth that isn't bound by any science. They used familiar pictures to show the revelation of the sovereign God within history.

Humanity Created

In these two accounts of the creation of humanity, one depicts a simultaneous creation of man and woman, while the other dramatizes the creation first of Adam and then the creation of Eve from Adam's rib. These two creation stories have caused much debate among biblical scholars and others through the years. In the simultaneous creation story, both sexes are depicted as on equal planes with one another; while the other seems to imply that since Adam was created first, that makes Eve of a lower status than him. They both are created in the "image of God." This implies that masculinity and femininity both derive from God, which means that God contains both maleness and femaleness in the divine being. God then is both father and mother as Creator. Some assert that Adam is superior to Eve because he was created first in one of the stories, but that argument falls flat when one has to acknowledge that animals were created before both of them. With that argument, does not that make animals superior to human beings? I don't think many people, if any, will support that view.

The word Hebrew word *Adam*, translated as Man, depicts more than an individual man; it reflects in the name, Adam, a sense of "community"—containing in that name both masculine and feminine characteristics. The name Adam reflects humanity at large. The argument that Eve is second to Adam because she was taken from his side fails when Old Testament scholars like Phyllis Trible note that Eve, being taken from Adam's side, denotes equality rather than inferior status. To be taken from Adam's side, she argues, speaks of equal standing—side by side. The word rendered "helpmeet" (King James Version) has also been translated as "partner." Trible argues further that being created last in this creation story signifies that Eve is the culmination of creation or the "crown of creation."[2] Those who want to place Eve on a level below Adam may have difficulty with this argument. I think the biblical writer or writers were striving to show that God created both man and woman to share in community together. One without the other is incomplete, or to use the Genesis wording, Adam was "lonely." God says that "it is not good for man [human beings] to be alone." God declares "aloneness" as "not good."

Eve is created to be the "fitting helper" or "partner" to bridge the chasm of loneliness. In other words, companionship or togetherness is essential for a person to function properly.

Created to Love

In the creation story, there is no indication of when this overcoming of loneliness is transformed into love. Sex is certainly not condemned, since the account indicates that Adam and Eve were created "to be fruitful and multiply and fill the earth" (1:26). Those who try to assert that sex is a result of sin ignore this reason for humans' creation. Some have assumed that since Adam and Eve did not have a child until they left the Garden of Eden, sex was a result of sin. This interpretation dishonors the biblical text. Sex was not evil but good and essential for the future of the human race. God was the original "matchmaker," and sex was an essential function of the relationship of companionship. The biblical writers do not give us an indication of when companionship becomes love or when love becomes companionship, nor is there any word about a "courtship" between the two humans. Surely all authentic love contains companionship or the significance of community or shared devotion to one another. Like all human relationships, surely Adam and Eve's experience was an evolving one as they got to know one another, and their relationship deepened into love and companionship. It seems that they slowly learned that life focuses primarily not around I/me but around we/us.

Disobedience

In Genesis 2:4b-17 and 3:1 and beyond, the writer gives us a scene where Adam and Eve are placed in a garden where two trees are of particular note—the "Tree of Life" and the "Tree of Knowledge." Nothing is said about the Tree of Life. It likely represents the fellowship Adam and Eve shared with God or a sign of the presence of God with them. The Tree of Knowledge contains fruit that God prohibits them from eating lest they die. The "talking serpent" enters the story and suggests that Eve should eat from this tree. Claus Westermann, the Heidelberg Old Testament scholar, believes the "snake" "is nothing more than the narrative symbol of the power of temptation."[3] When Eve responds that they are told they can eat from any of the other trees but are not to eat from this tree, the serpent slyly replies that they will not die but will be like God. They are told that their eyes will be opened, and they will know good and evil. Eve succumbs and eats from the tree and then offers some of the fruit to Adam, who also eats; but they, like the serpent told them, do not die. Their knowledge of good and evil now reveals to them that they are naked. Some have suggested that Adam and Eve were perfect before "the Fall" in the Garden of Eden. But when God created them, the Scriptures described God as saying they were "good," not perfect. They, like we are, were created with the possibility of choosing good or evil. Neither we nor they were or are perfect. Dietrich Bonhoeffer interprets their sin in this light: "It is revolt, it is the creature's departure from the attitude which is the only possible attitude for him, it is the creature's becoming Creator, it is the destruction of creatureliness. It is the fall from being held in creatureliness."[4] It is our human sin to want to be like God, to be the Creator. It is our "God almightiness."

When Adam and Eve are confronted by God, with what they have done by eating from the forbidden Tree of Knowledge, they acknowledge what they have done. Eve blames the serpent for deceiving her, while Adam blames the woman. Adam seeks to place the blame and responsibility on Eve even though he ate of the tree with his own free will. Neither were forced to eat from the tree but chose to do so on their own. Realistically, they might try to blame each other or someone/something else, but each one was morally responsible for their own disobedience. But they do not die, as the serpent said. Instead, God responds to their disobedience in three ways: First, the serpent is cursed to crawl on its belly in the future and is depicted as the least of all species, and enmity will be established between the serpent and the woman. Second, Adam will have to labor by the sweat of his brow for food to eat, and, as he was created from dust, to dust he will return. Third, Eve will find her childbearing more painful, and her desire will be for her husband who will rule over her.

On leaving the garden, God does not punish them with death but shows mercy. God gives the woman a name, Eve—the mother of all living creatures—and clothes both humans with garments of skins as they depart.

The Concept of a Fall

Through the ages, many have seen Genesis 3 as evidence of the "Fall of Man." Milton based his epic poem, *Paradise Lost*, on this passage. Augustine, Luther, Calvin, Wesley, and countless other theologians have seen Adam's disobedience as the "Fall" of the human race or the source of "original sin." This belief asserts that because of Adam's disobedience, humanity has been hopelessly corrupted, and we are all alienated from obeying God. These scholars traced their interpretation also to the Apostle Paul's writing in Romans 5:12-21, especially verse 12: "Therefore, just as sin came into the world through one man, and death came through sin, and so death spread to all because all have sinned . . . ." The Old Testament scholar Walter Brueggemann thinks that Paul was concerned not with the origin of evil, sin, or death but with the "proclamation of good news" about Jesus Christ. He rejects the view that this passage in Genesis 3 is to be seen as an explanation for the theoretical or abstract origin of evil, sin, or death.[5] The theologian Emil Brunner, whose work I read in seminary many years ago, affirmed this view long before the writings of Brueggemann, declaring that attributing the doctrine of the Fall of Adam as "the transference of his sin to the succeeding generations is following a method which is in no sense Biblical."[6]

Terence Fretheim, professor of Old Testament at Luther Northwestern Theological Seminary, sees the Fall metaphor as a primary image of "separation, estrangement, alienation, and displacement" but also sees it "in fundamental ways to reflect the character of human life in every age, which is filled with disharmonious relationships at all levels of life."[7] In the earlier Interpreter's Bible series, Walter Russell Bowie wrote, "The truth of the wonderful old drama of Eden is not that we are accounted evil because somebody before us did evil. The truth dramatized there is this: Human nature, made to go God's way, has an inveterate tendency to listen to the temptation to go its own way, and the rebellious way must have an evil end."[8] This ancient narrative reminds us that our basic sin is mistrusting God and relying on our own resources apart from God. And unfortunately, this story seems to be repeated down through the ages.

To me, the story of the Fall of Adam is a "parable" of the "fall" of each of us. Every person experiences their own personal "disobedience" to God. I am guilty, and you are guilty, not because Adam and Eve fell but because you and I made our own decision to be disobedient to God. My fall may have occurred when, as a child, I told my mother or father a lie about something I had done. My fall may have happened when I took some small item from the Ten Cent Store when I was young, put it in my pocket, and walked out of the store without paying for it, or when my eyes fell on another student's paper during a test. You and I may not recall the exact moment, but for each of us there was a moment of deciding between right or wrong, and we made the erroneous choice, and our "fall" occurred. Brunner expresses this truth this way: "If we were forced to say at what point the Fall takes place in the life of the individual person, then I suppose we might say this: it is the moment when the child first becomes conscious of himself as an 'I', and when he actually expresses it."[9] The "I" in me in that moment takes the "fruit" from the Tree of Knowledge of Good and Evil.

Taking the Genesis account literally and blaming all the rest of humanity for something that happened centuries ago in the Fall of Adam is not only unfair but a description of God that makes God capricious and cruel. You and I, I believe, are responsible for our own sins and not for Adam or Eve's disobedience. The story is not history but parabolic, mythological, or allegorical. It is the story of Everyone. At some point in our journey through life, we each are confronted to decide between good and evil, right or wrong, truth or lie. And we make the wrong decision.

A Family Model

After leaving the Garden of Eden, Adam and Eve begin their family. I have read almost nothing about the fact that Adam and Eve had children and started the first family. We do not read what they did after they left the garden and how they raised their food, where they lived, or how they evolved in their personal relationship. The writer was not interested in these matters, but to me, they raise stimulating questions. The couple has two children; one son, Abel, was a shepherd, and the other, Cain, was a farmer. When you have a son who kills his brother, that indicates to me that the family was a little dysfunctional. In no way does the writer try to depict an ideal family; he reveals the family as they were—striving toward wholeness with flawed understanding, misunderstanding, jealousy, rage, selfishness, confusion, immaturity, and normal flaws of humanity reaching toward maturity.

When Cain was asked what happened to his brother, he responded with "Am I my brother's keeper?" No, he was not his brother's keeper, but he was his brother's brother. His sin of killing his brother led to his own rejection and isolation by his family. Thus, to me, their grief was compounded by this tragedy. They lost a son by death and another by rejection. This is a sad commentary on family relations and is certainly not a model for good family relationships. The Bible begins its story about humanity with the sharing of the dispute and jealousy within a family and the inability of brothers to get along with each other to the extent that it leads to tragedy and broken relationships.

Grief

The account also addresses the grief that Adam and Eve must have experienced at the death of a son and the grief of fragmented family relationships. Later the writer acknowledges the death of Adam, which must have caused grief in the life of Eve, although this is not mentioned in the text. The text also does not mention the death of Eve or how either of them dealt with any of their losses. Nevertheless, this is a reminder of the reality of grief in any family relationship.

Lessons for Today

What are some lessons for today that we can learn from this ancient story? First, we affirm that God is the source of the human race. I believe that the Scriptures bear witness to God as Creator and sovereign Lord. However, I do not have to accept the Genesis accounts as objective historical narrative in order to do this. The writers were expressing in symbolic and parabolic language an eternal insight about God's nature: God is Creator. It is not necessary, either, for me to accept as normative or final the conceptual images with which they express this truth. The scientific images and views may change from one generation to the next, but God remains Creator. Just because we no longer tend sheep in our town does not mean that God is not the Good Shepherd. We may have to use a different image now to express this truth, such as Comforter, Guide, or Director. In his book *God Is for Real, Man*, Carl F. Burke has related the way some young people in the tough part of an inner city have pictured God. Some of the spiritual truths are formed in ways that may seem novel or repulsive to some, but they have meaning to those people. The Shepherd of the Twenty-third Psalm is vivid: "The Lord is like my probation officer." They use phrases like "God is Mr. Big." Or the good Samaritan is a "real cool square." The Pharisee and the tax collector are called "The Wheel and the Character." To some this seems heretical and offensive, but to the folks Burke knows, the language makes God and the Bible real. They are still speaking about the same Bible and the same God, but they use words that are understandable to them.

Second, God created humanity, and sexuality is an authentic part of that creation. Sex is not evil, not the result of any Fall of Adam, but is a natural function for men and women in creation. Sex, like any human act, can be misused and abused, but that does not negate its proper function. We were created for love and companionship; no life is complete in itself but yearns for community with another life for genuine fulfillment.

Third, human beings sin and are disobedient to God by their own choices and not as the result of Adam's sin. Adam and Eve's disobedience is symbolic of everyone's personal "fall." Adam and Eve were created with the ability to choose good or evil, just as we are. Their choice was a sign of the reality that all of us, at some point in our lives, make a choice to eat "fruit" from some forbidden Tree of Knowledge that results in our sinning. God is merciful and will forgive us, but all people sin.

Fourth, family is important. The love that blossoms into companionship and community often includes children. The Genesis story reminds us that all families may have struggles, conflicts, misunderstandings, and dysfunctions, but we strive for wholeness, love, and shared community. There may be difficult times, but family love can help us meet the tragedies and conflicts that may arise.

Fifth, grief is a normal reality that will affect us all at some time. It may be the death of a child, parent, spouse, or friend, but no one avoids this tragedy in their journey through life. Death is a part of life that no one can avoid or escape. We may try to ignore it or disguise it, but it will not go away. Grief often leads to traumatized couples or people who have displaced anger, guilt, regrets, denial, and other feelings. We must learn how to live with death—our own and others' whom we love.

Crying is a normal, healthy emotional outlet for any person suffering from a grief experience. Unfortunately, our society has tried to suppress this common reaction by saying, "Don't break down now; you know he wouldn't want that." "Don't cry anymore; that won't bring your mother back." "Come on, son; be a man now, and don't cry." The deep ache, sore hurt, and bottled-up feelings need to be expressed, and no mourner needs to feel any sense of apology or disgrace for weeping. Do so unashamedly—in the privacy of your room, on the shoulder of a relative or friend, wherever there are understanding friends. Feel free to express your grief. The Chinese have a proverb: "If you do not weep outwardly, you will weep inwardly." Daniel Bagby, professor emeritus of the Theodore F. Adams Pastoral Care Chair at the Baptist Theological Seminary in Richmond, Virginia, has affirmed strongly the healing and releasing power of tears:

> Our tears, then, are not rude interruptions in the healing of our lives; in fact they are allies in the journey to cleansing and releasing. Sometimes we need to cry in order to "link up" with our next step of recovery and hope. Tears, then, are physical stepping stones on the journey of renewal. The release and balance they provide us

are essential to our personal survival and well-being. They bring us hope; they remind us that failure is not the last word.[10]

The big question of "why" did God allow or cause such a thing raises its voice often in the struggle with death. Harold Kushner, who lost his fourteen-year-old son to the disease progeria, reminds us in his book *When Bad Things Happen to Good People* that death, illness, and tragedy are a natural part of life and are not something we should blame on God, nor does God make exceptions for good people. Two of my books, *Facing Grief and Death: Living with Dying* and *A Positive Word for Christian Lamenting*, offer practical suggestions for confronting such crises.[11] The support of family and friends is essential in facing grief, but ultimately we lean in trust on God, who comforts us with divine assurance of life after death through Christ our Lord.

We need to confront grief with the assurance of the promises of Jesus: "So you have sorrow now, but I will see you again and your hearts will rejoice, and no one will take your joy from you" (John 16:22). "Peace I leave with you; my peace I give to you; not as the world gives do I give to you. Let not your hearts be troubled, neither let them be afraid" (John 14:27).

A boy was helping his father bring in some wood for the fire, and he was struggling under the weight of a heavy load. "Why don't you use all your strength?" the father asked. "I am," the little lad responded, feeling dejected. "No, you're not," declared the father, "You have not asked me to help you." And he reached down and lifted both the boy and log in his arms. No one has ever used all of their strength until they have drawn on the source of all strength itself—the eternal God. "Cast your burden on the LORD, and he will sustain you" (Ps 55:22).

Abraham: A Journey of Faith

Genesis 12:1-3; 22:1-18

Twenty-two years after World War I ended, Hollywood producers decided to make a movie about one of the heroes of that war, Sergeant York. This young man was from the mountains of Tennessee. Before they made the movie, the producers wanted to find out what had happened to the heroes who were part of the squad under Sergeant York in the Aragon Forest. There they had darted tree to tree and through the grain fields under heavy machine-gun fire. In this encounter, the squad killed 25 German soldiers and captured 163 more. The movie producers discovered that two of these soldiers were now farming in the mountains of Tennessee. As for the rest of them, one was working in a mill, and one was a night watchman in the mill. One drove a truck in Massachusetts; one was in a veteran's home; and two were simply drifters. The last one they tried to contact lived in a small ramshackle shack in the mountains of Tennessee. They knocked on his door, and he refused to answer.

The question that comes to our minds is, "What happened to these men?" Look at some of them now. What made the difference? Down through the ages, people have often asked, "What makes a hero? Why does a person do something heroic in a particular situation and then later doesn't seem able to do anything else worthwhile?" William Archer wrote a parody based on Peter Seeger's song a few years ago in which he raised the following questions:

Where have all the heroes gone, long time missing?

Where have all the heroes gone, a long time ago?
Where have all the heroes gone? They've lost their haloes one by
   one;
When will we ever learn? When will we ever learn?[1]

When we look around us in our day and age, we discover that it is difficult to find many heroes. The heroes for most of our young people today are rock singers, TV and movie stars, and ball players; teenagers might add gamers or creators on YouTube and TikTok. When you get beyond that, many young people have difficulty naming anybody else that is a hero to them. But be honest: if you had to talk about the heroes in your own life, whom would you mention? Whom would you list as the great heroes in our country or in the world? Since many of us have so much difficulty doing that, I decided to help us focus on some heroes—not contemporary heroes but heroes from the past. I want us to look at some of the great Old Testament heroes of the faith.

Father of Our Faith

Let's look at the "great patriarch" and "Father of our Faith," Abraham. The faith of Abraham is the stream from which three great religious heritages have come—Islam, Judaism, and Christianity. The Abraham narrative begins in Genesis 11:26 and concludes with 25:18, fourteen chapters. In his book *Messengers of God*, Elie Wiesel wrote these lines:

Abraham: the first enemy of idolatry. The first angry young man. The first rebel to rise up against the "establishment," society and authority. The first to demystify official taboos and suspend ritual prohibitions. The first to reject civilization in order to form a minority of one. The first believer, the first one to suffer for his belief. Alone against the world, he declared himself free. Alone against the world, he braved the fire and the mob, affirming that God is one and present wherever His name is invoked.[2]

Abraham's Call

Abraham received a call from God to a pioneering journey. This is a strange call when we take time to consider it. The call from God addressed Abraham in this way: "Abraham, get up from where you are, and I want you to go to someplace else, but I am not going to tell you where that is yet. You just start traveling. Strike your tent and move on." This call challenged Abraham to launch out into the deep, lift anchor and sail, get moving. For those of us who need security, permanence, and the comforts of home, that would sound like a strange call and one that many of us, especially today, would not want to hear. I am not so sure Abraham wanted to hear that kind of demand either. The Old Testament scholar Jürgen Moltmann called Abraham the beginning point of "exodus religion." He was called to be on the move, constantly wandering.

Abraham's call to be a pioneer was also a call to separate. He was instructed, "Leave your kinspeople, your land, and your father." Many people are deeply devoted to their families, so to forsake family and one's country are not easily heeded demands. But with God's revelation came this demand to journey: "Leave your family and homeland and go wherever I will direct you." H. Wheeler Robinson has suggested that rather than just the story of an isolated individual, the patriarch Abraham may represent "a corporate personality."[3] The migration had already begun under Terah, Abraham's father. Then, upon the death of Terah at Haran (Gen 11:32), Abraham, the eldest son, assumed leadership of the clan. In one place, for example, the writer of Genesis notes that Abraham rescued Lot with 318 "trained men" (Gen 14:14). Abraham's journey, then, was not that of an isolated individual but of the leader of a tribe of people who were willing to follow God wherever God led them.

Two Symbols

In Abraham's life there were two central symbols—the altar and the tent. The altar was the symbol of his worship of God. Everywhere he went he built an altar and worshiped God Almighty. Abraham's journey was a pilgrimage in which he learned that his God, known only as "El Shaddai," God Almighty, was not merely a tribal god limited to a specific place but the one God who was universal and not limited by space or time. The migration may have been seen by some as a desire for better pasture lands or to avoid other desert tribes, but the underlying motive for Abraham was obedience to the call of God.

His living in a tent was symbolic that he was a sojourner. The writer of the book of Hebrews notes the faith of Abraham in these words: "He went out not knowing where he was to go. By faith he sojourned in the land of promise, as in a foreign land, living in tents with Isaac and Jacob, heirs with him of the same promise. For he looked forward to the city which has foundations, whose builder and maker is God" (Heb 11:8-10).

The Blessing of Abraham

Note first, Abraham began his journey at God's command, but he was also assured that God promised him a blessing. He was told that if he would obey God and follow him, he would be blessed, and he would be a blessing to others. What was this blessing? A part of his blessing, the greatest part, was his own sense of the presence of God. He had a personal relationship with the God whom he followed faithfully. God never promised him a life void of pain and struggle, but this blessing was an inner peace, a sense of security that enabled him to face the struggles and difficulties he encountered along his journey.

Myron C. Madden recounts an experience he had with a woman he was asked to visit in the hospital at the birth of her new daughter. After talking a while, he asked her the name of her new child. She said, "I named her *I Am*." He asked her how she arrived at that name. "You ought to know, Reverend. I got it from the Bible," she said. He agreed with that insight but still asked her again, "But I wonder why you named her *I Am*?" "There are so many people out here," she responded, "who don't know who they are. I thought I would give her a head start."[4]

"I Am." Well, the great God who said, "I Am" gave to Abraham that same sense of inner confidence to face the circumstances in which he found himself. We all need that kind of head start to face the struggles of life.

Abraham was also told that he would be a blessing to others. He was blessed not for some selfish end but to touch the lives of others. He was blessed to become the father of many nations. Through his son Ishmael, the Arab nation was begun. Through his son Isaac, the nation of Israel—the Jews—came into existence, and out of Israel came the resurrected Christ on whom the church was founded. Thousands and thousands of people have been blessed because of Abraham. When Abraham received God's revelation and was blessed by God, his name was changed from Abram (honored father) to Abraham (father of a multitude).

Our Call to Be a Blessing

Like Abraham, we too have been called to be a blessing to others. We all know of people who have blessed us by their love, concern, guidance, encouragement, and support. We have been blessed by their examples and challenged to bless others because of their impact on our lives.

I heard about a young man who was going off to college for the first time and struggled to express his appreciation to his parents for the sacrifices they had made for him to go and the investment they had made in him through their love and guidance. "How can I ever pay you back for what you have done?" he asked. "Son, don't be concerned about that," his father replied. "You in turn will express your love to your own children." "Oh no, I'll pay you back," the son protested. "No, son," his mother said gently. "Remember that you do not need to pay us back for our love. You can't pay it back. It is something that you can only pass on to your own children. You look forward, not backward. You can't pay it back but only pass it on."

Abraham was blessed by becoming a blessing to others. Having experienced the presence of God, Abraham was called to go on a journey with only faith in God as his primary source of strength. But with a vision in his head and a heart filled with obedience, he began a journey to sow the seeds to bless the nations of the earth. We, like Abraham, have been called to be men and women of the Way—Christ's way. He has called us to come out of the world and be separate. He calls us to be different, to be the salt of the earth and the light of the world. If we are going to follow the Christlike way, then we have to separate ourselves from the ways of the world and model ourselves after Christ. There are times when we need to hear the same command Abraham heard: "Go from your country and your kindred and your father's house." When we hear God's voice calling us, we in obedience must separate ourselves and then step forward in faith.

A Journey Filled with Struggles

Second, notice that Abraham's faith journey was often filled with struggle. Too many people think that following God always fills our lives with sweetness and light. These people naively assume that Christians will have an easy road to travel and that the blessing of God means we will never have difficulties or struggles. But look at the great Old Testament and New Testament characters and note that they often faced lonely, hard, and trying times.

To love and follow God is often a calling not to an easy way but to a difficult one. Abraham did not know how God would fulfill his promise since his wife Sarah was childless. When Abraham journeyed into the land that God promised him, he discovered that it was occupied by others, like the Canaanites. Often Abraham found his tribe engaged in battle with them. Soon after he arrived in Palestine, Abraham found himself amid a national famine. What did he do? Why, he got on his camel and took off for Egypt. This man who had followed God to the promised land by faith immediately encountered difficulties. When he did, he fled to the delta of Egypt. Abraham took the typical approach that many take when they face problems. What is the answer? To run from them. When Abraham's dream seemed evasive, he ran to Egypt. There the man of great faith engaged in deception. At this moment, Abraham failed to use his faith. For a short while, he did not believe the promise.

Abraham's wife, Sarah, was a beautiful woman. He was afraid that her beauty would cause the Egyptians to kill him so they could possess her. Therefore, he told her, "Let's pretend that you are my sister. If Pharaoh and other Egyptian leaders think you are my sister, my life will be spared." Pharaoh was impressed by Sarah, and Abraham let him take her into his household as his wife. Literally speaking, Sarah was Abraham's half-sister, but she was also his wife. He committed this sin simply to protect himself. He revealed a weakness in his faith. Because of Abraham's sin, God sent a plague upon Pharaoh's house. Pharaoh confronted Abraham when he realized that Sarah was his wife and told him, "Take your wife and leave." Why did Abraham commit this sin? Because he was concerned for his own safety and demonstrated little concern for his wife. Without question, this act showed a lack of faith.

The episode clearly reveals Abraham's humanity. Our father in the faith had clay feet. Even this man of great faith, through whom nations would come into existence, showed his own weakness. This act showed that Abraham was a fellow, weak human being who, like all the rest of us, struggled to understand God and life. He fell not at his weakest point but at his strongest. Abraham was noted for his faith, yet that was the very place where he showed a weakness. He failed to have enough faith in the midst of famine and fled to Egypt. When he got to Egypt, his faith failed him again as he lied to protect himself. He had left all to follow God to have his destiny fulfilled, but he could not trust God in this segment of his journey. The first time he met difficulties, Abraham revealed an insecure faith. He stumbled and fell into sin.

Not a Perfect Instrument

Abraham's story reminds us that God doesn't need perfect instruments to do his work. God has never had perfect instruments. God has always had to work through imperfect people. Look at the imperfect vessels he has used through the centuries—Isaac, Jacob, David, Saul who became the Apostle Paul, and countless others. God continues to work through you and me. None of us is perfect. All of us are fragile instruments, yet God still uses us in his kingdom.

Dwight L. Moody was led to Christ by a layman named Edward Kimball. Later when Moody began to preach, he was often criticized for his poor grammar and his lack of education. He would readily acknowledge his limitations, but he would then remind those who criticized him that "I am using my gifts for Christ. I have dedicated all that I have to him. What are you doing for him with your gifts?"

It is easy to criticize the work others do for Christ. But the question each of us needs to ask is, "What am I doing in ministry for Christ?" Abraham's sin reminds us that God can use all kinds of instruments, and they do not have to be perfect.

Abraham's Call for Sacrifice

Third, Abraham's journey of faith called for sacrifice. As we look at Abraham's story, we discover that along his whole journey he had to combat difficulties and struggles. It was never easy. He experienced famine and had a wife who was childless. According to this story, when Abraham was a hundred years old, his wife gave birth to their only child together, Isaac. This child was the dear and bright spot of their lives. The twenty-second chapter of Genesis is one of the best known in the narrative about Abraham. But many people find the theology in this story difficult. God's demand for Abraham to make the supreme sacrifice of his own son is repugnant to us today. Today, if somebody attempted to commit such an act, they would be arrested for attempted murder and put in jail. We would consider such an act inhumane. How could God command a father to kill his own son?

Scholars, ministers, and laypeople have wrestled with this passage in an effort to come to grips with its meaning. Some have interpreted this account as a parable, like the story of the prodigal son in Jesus' parable. This story as a parable was told to show the divine disapproval of human sacrifice. The human sacrifice of infants, especially the firstborn child, was common in this ancient time. The pagan worship practices of the Canaanites reveal that they often practiced the sacrifice of newborn infants. Archaeologists in excavations at Gezer discovered a cemetery with clay jars containing the bones of babies who had been sacrificed to their gods. Unfortunately, human sacrifice was also a practice in Israel and did not end until the seventh or eighth centuries BCE (Isa 57:5; Mic 6:7; Jer 7:31). Some believe that this story was intended to end the practice of human sacrifice.

Scholar G. Henton Davies of Regent Park College, Oxford, England, got in a great deal of trouble with Southern Baptists several years ago when he stated in his Genesis commentary that God has never asked anybody to do anything that goes against God's own character. He believed that no such command could have come from God but was "the climax of the psychology of his [the individual's] life."[5] The question is, "Was this feeling something Abraham perceived within his own mind, or was it at the direction of God?" Several years ago, the famous TV evangelist Oral Roberts stated that God told him that if he didn't raise a certain amount of money by a certain date, God was going to take him home. What a mockery this is to an understanding of the nature of God. Did God tell Roberts to do this, or did it arise out of his own feelings? Sometimes people make claims for God that come out of their own consciousness. I do not believe that God demands from us anything that is morally wrong. Ralph Elliott has expressed this concept in these powerful words:

> God does not test a man of faith with a command to do something that is morally wrong and contrary to the character of God. In fact, one of the strongest statements in the Old Testament for ascertaining whether something is the will or word or command of God is to ask whether it is in keeping with the character of God (Deut 13:1ff).[6]

We must remember that this story took place four thousand years ago. Abraham's narrative depicted an occurrence that happened two thousand years before Christ. Remember that this was a primitive society in which human sacrifice was not seen as immoral. Infant sacrifice was not seen as wrong. It was a part of the worship practice of many in the ancient world.

A Test of Faith

No matter how you may want to interpret Abraham's motivation for this act, the Genesis writer is seeking to tell us that it came to Abraham as a great test of his faith and that his obedience brought him freedom and blessing. Whether the motivation arose within his own heart or came from God, it was a test of his faith. Out of a heart filled with anguish, Abraham was asked to sacrifice his dearest possession, his own son. Gerhard Von Rad, the noted Old Testament scholar, has suggested that this test came as a challenge for Abraham to understand that Isaac, the gift of promise, was a pure gift from God. Abraham was tested by God to see if he was willing to give up God's gift of promise for his destiny.[7] The challenge was for him to see that all of his life was a gift and not the result of something he had achieved himself. Isaac was a gift to him from God. Would he lose the promise of God by his unwillingness to give up what he loved the most? If he sacrificed Isaac, how could the promise be realized? It was a confusing, contradictory command.

Wrestle for a moment with the literal account of this story. It seems strange that after Abraham received the command to sacrifice his son, there was no record of any argument from him or the turmoil that went on within his soul. We also have no discussion of Isaac's reaction to this command that he be a sacrifice, other than the one question: "Where is the lamb?" Abraham responded, "The LORD will provide." And Abraham himself carried the material to make the fire as well as the knife, the dangerous part of the load. His son bore only the wood, the portion of the sacrificial preparations that could not harm him.

Danish philosopher Søren Kierkegaard, in his book *Fear and Trembling*, presented several imaginary conversations that may have taken place between Abraham and Isaac. His imaginary conversations reflect their internal conflict, fear, terror, and anger, but the biblical account gives us no evidence of the struggle within either person. After the father indicated to his son that he was to be the sacrifice, the young son obviously had to let himself be bound willingly by his father. Did Abraham then bend over his son and gently kiss him before he raised his knife to sacrifice him? Suddenly the voice of the angel of the Lord stopped him: "Do not lay your hand on the lad or do anything to him; for now, I know that you fear God."

Our Own Testing

What do we make of this? Many of us are uncomfortable with the notion of God "testing" anyone. But Walter Brueggemann reminds us that this same issue is seen in the New Testament as well as the

Old Testament and is nowhere more apparent than in the prayer of Jesus when he taught his disciples to pray, "lead us not into temptation"—the time of testing. The early church also experienced times of testing (Mark 13:9-13; 1 Pet 1:7; 2 Pet 2:9).[8] The test of Abraham's faith was the challenge to see if he was willing to give up the hope of his destiny, which had been promised through the son he was asked to sacrifice. Was he willing to give up everything and trust God completely? That was a tough test. Elie Wiesel, the Jewish writer who was sent as a child to Auschwitz and Buchenwald by the Germans, has observed that

> of all the biblical tales, the one about Isaac is perhaps the most timeless and most relevant to our generation. We have known Jews who, like Abraham, witnessed the death of their children . . . and some who went mad when they saw their father disappear on the altar, with the altar, in a blazing fire whose flames reached into the highest heaven.[9]

God Provides

This story began with Abraham's faith being tested by God, but it ends with God providing. To believe that God would provide a way other than the sacrifice of his son was also an act of faith. Abraham had taken the ultimate test and had been faithful. Abraham looked around and found a ram caught by his horns in a thicket. God did provide indeed. The lamb became a substitute offering.

Does Moriah in a faint way point to Calvary, where centuries later God offered his only begotten Son, whom he deeply loved? What he did not expect from Abraham he willingly gave to redeem the world. Was the faithfulness of Abraham a dim glimpse of the costly sacrifice of God, who willingly surrendered his Son for our salvation? Paul expressed God's love and sacrifice in these words: "He who did not spare his Son but gave him up for us all" (Rom 8:32).

I don't think for a moment that God is going to ask you and me to sacrifice our children. That is not the kind of God we worship today. But you and I do need to understand that we may have something in our lives that symbolizes Isaac and has taken the place that rightfully belongs to God. What are the things in your life and mine that are so precious to us that we are unwilling to let them go and to follow God? Abraham had to learn that Isaac was not his possession but God's gift. He faced what all of us must face: the temptation to let someone else or something else take first place instead of God. God demands our ultimate loyalty. Many of us cling to other things and are unwilling to let them go. They take first place in our lives instead of God. God asks each of us to give our lives fully and completely to him. I wonder how many of us have been willing to do that? What symbolizes the Isaac in your life?

When Bishop Williams S. Lewis was in China many years ago, he asked a young Chinese man, who had given up an important government position, why he decided to enter the ministry. The young man responded,

> During the Boxer uprising, I lived in an inland village where there was a temple for devil worship. The Christians were led by the soldiers to that temple and ordered to renounce their religion and bow before the devil image or be executed. I saw 163 of my townsmen walk by the devil god with heads erect, when a little bow would have saved their lives—then out to a great beam over which they placed their heads for the swift stroke of the executioner's sword that sent their heads rolling in the dust. My father was one of that number. It was the unshaken integrity of their faith that thrilled me and gave me a longing for the new life. I must go back and tell my fellow townsmen of Christ, who loves them, and of his power to save.

Abraham stands as a model of faithfulness. Although he was human and at times his faith showed signs of weakness like that of all people, he withstood the supreme test of his faith. He slowly came to realize that all of life was a gift from God. This awareness causes us to remember that we ultimately live by faith in the eternal God who is the giver of all good gifts. Like Abraham, I hope that each of us will learn to be more willing to serve God and dedicate our all to him as we journey in our pilgrimage through life by faith in him.

Jacob: Wrestling to Find His Place

Genesis 27:1-27; 32:24-31

"Jacob was left alone, and a man wrestled with him till daybreak."

Biblical scholars, rabbis, poets, and philosophers have tried to interpret this strange and mysterious encounter at Jabbok. Who was the stranger with whom Jacob wrestled? Was he the demon of Jacob's own conscience or the ghost of the past in the form of Esau or Isaac? Was Jacob's past catching up with him? Was the future descending upon him? Why would the stranger not reveal his name? What a story—a man and an angel wrestling all night!

Who was this stranger Jacob met at the River Jabbok? For centuries, all kinds of people have attempted to understand its meaning. What does it mean to wrestle all night with someone who represents God? But you and I know that kind of struggle ourselves, don't we? Who among us has not had a time of crisis in life where we had to struggle all night until dawn to sense God's blessing? Does Jacob's struggle not symbolize the story of every person struggling with a demon or angel from their past or future until each is blessed?

Jacob Had Experienced Conflict Before

Jacob was no stranger to conflict. He had known struggle all his life. Even before he was born, he was engaged in a wrestling match with his twin brother. His twin brother Esau—the red-haired one—was born first, but Jacob came out of his mother's womb hanging on

Esau's heel as though he were saying, "You ought not to be first, but me!" Nevertheless, Esau was born first, and Jacob, the second son, who was born only a few moments later, was named "the one who catches the heel," "the supplanter," or "the trickster."

Jacob was no stranger to wrestling matches. Here beside the River Jabbok, he is waiting to see his brother again the next morning. It has been twenty years since he laid eyes on his brother. To be honest, he is not so enthusiastic about their encounter. The last time he saw his brother, Esau wanted to kill him. And Jacob is not sure what this meeting will bring to pass. He is not looking forward to this reunion. Storm clouds from the past cast long, dark shadows. On the dark night before meeting with Esau, he wrestles within . . . and so he should.

Look with me at Jacob's lifelong wrestling match with others. Jacob and his twin brother Esau were born to Abraham's son Isaac and his wife Rebekah. When he and his brother were much younger, Esau, who was the outdoorsman and hunter and his father's favorite, came in exhausted and hungry one day. Jacob was the quieter of the two, the homebody, and his mother's favorite son. Jacob had a pot of lentil broth cooking on the fire. His brother pleaded for something to eat. Jacob saw how hungry and exhausted his brother was and said, "Well, you can have something to eat if you will promise to give me your birthright." What a demand! According to Hebrew tradition, the firstborn child was supposed to receive a double portion of his father's goods at his death. "Swear to me that you will give me your birthright," Jacob said. For a bowl of broth? It sounds absurd.

But Esau threw his inheritance aside and said, "I am too hungry. Give me food to eat now." He rejected his right as the firstborn in exchange for the physical satisfaction of the moment. He was unable to wait. He wanted food immediately! We all know that struggle. We see this tendency in other individuals and in ourselves. Our physical appetites overpower us, and we stumble and fall into sin. We don't have the ability to wait. We want instant satisfaction. We cannot patiently wait for something we desire. We want our demands met now.

Years passed, and Isaac, the son of Abraham, became old and blind. He called from his tent for his son, Esau. He asked him to kill his favorite game and told him that he would then give Esau his final blessing. Isaac either thought he was dying or he really was dying. It is doubtful that he was too near death, since he was well enough to want something to eat, and he also lived for a while after this episode.

Esau rushed off to find some meat for his father. He had to hunt it, kill it, and then cook it. That would take quite a while. Rebekah had been listening to this conversation and saw an opportunity to get her way for her favorite son. She went to Jacob and told him what Isaac had said. She instructed Jacob to kill two goats and prepare them for his father. She told him to put some skins of the goats on his hands and on the nape of his neck, so he would feel hairy like his brother. Then she instructed him to put on his brother's clothes. "Your old blind father will not know that you are not Esau," she says.

Remember that this is Isaac's own wife telling their son to do this! I don't know about you, but it seems to me that the idea of deceiving a blind old man is a clear indication of a deep weakness in the character of both mother and son. Jacob followed his mother's instructions and entered his father's tent with the prepared dish. Luther observed, "If it had been me, I'd have dropped the dish!" And probably you and I would have, too. But not Jacob. He was a cunning deceiver. Even in his youth he revealed that he had the ability to be deceptive. When his father asked him how he got back so quickly from the hunt, he lied several times and told him that Isaac's God had led him to find the animal; this was using their religion in a profane way.

A Stolen Blessing

But Jacob was not the first or the last to do that. He, like others, dragged God into the story and said that God had guided him in a certain way. It's hard to argue with folks who say that God guided them or told them to do something.

Isaac seemed unsure that the person in his tent was Esau. He asked him several times if he were his son Esau. But after he smelled his clothes, which had the outdoor smell of Esau, and felt the heavy hair on his neck and hands, he was assured that this was his older son and he blessed him. Here is the blessing:

> God give you dew from heaven and the riches of the earth, corn, and new wine and plenty. People shall serve you, nations bow down to you. Be lord over your brothers: may your mother's sons bow down to you. A curse upon those who curse you; and a blessing to those who bless you. (Gen 27:28-29, NEB)

That is quite a blessing. When Esau came in later and realized what had happened, he asked his father, "Do you not have another blessing that you can give me?" The blessing that Isaac gave Esau seemed almost like a curse.

Parents Who Fail to Bless their Children

Who among us does not want the blessing of their father or mother? How many young people or older people today still struggle with the fact that they have never felt the approval—the blessing, the affirmation—of a parent? Their lives have been crippled emotionally because they have never heard their parent say, "I love you"; "I care for you"; "I want you to succeed"; "You have my blessing." These people spend their whole lives competing and being combative to try to earn a blessing. Usually they never do. Of course, we know that they cannot. Some parent has withheld that blessing. They have been unwilling to embrace their son or daughter and bless them with their love.

When Esau realized what his brother had done, he was furious. He held his anger in for a while, but he said that when their father Isaac died, he would kill Jacob. Rebekah came rushing to her favorite son and said, "Esau is very angry right now. But let me tell you what to do. My brother, your uncle, lives over in Haran. Go stay with your uncle Laban until your brother gets over his anger. Then you can come back home."

Twenty years passed! Rebekah did not know that she was sending her favorite son away, never to see him again. She was willing to use any means possible to get the end that she desired for her son. She did not realize that her action would take him away from her. Jacob had to suffer the consequence of what he had done, and one of the consequences was never to see his mother or father alive again. His action alienated him from his brother, and Esau's anger trailed him down through the years.

Jacob Flees from Home and Dreams

A solitary figure, Jacob, crossed a barren desert. He had no caravan with him and no camels loaded down with valuable goods. He kept looking back over his shoulder to see if Esau was following him. He had cheated his brother and lied to his father. Did the barren desert remind him of his own deep sense of sin? Finally, he fell exhausted and collapsed into a deep sleep. Since he had so few possessions, he pulled up a rock for a pillow. While he slept, Jacob dreamed. In his dream he saw a ziggurat like the ones he may have seen in Mesopotamia. This ziggurat looked like a stairwell or ramp that reached up to heaven. This image was not like a ladder leaning against a house. It looked more like a stair-step ramp that went from the ground to heaven. Angels came down the steps and disclosed the mystery, wonder, and presence of God to Jacob. He had not expected this revelation, and he was terrified by the experience. When he woke he said, "I didn't know that this was the gateway to heaven."

Why Did Jacob Have This Dream?

I don't know why God appeared to Jacob of all people. As hard as we look, there is nothing in the biblical record to indicate that Jacob was religious. Yes, he was the grandson of Abraham, but we have a lot of sons of ministers, missionaries, and all kinds of folks who may not be religious at all. Being the son, grandson, or daughter doesn't guarantee that a person will be religious. Religion does not come by the process of osmosis. The only time Jacob used the name of God was when he was trying to trick Isaac into thinking he was his brother Esau. "Your God," Jacob said, "has enabled me to find this meat."

That statement bothered me at first. How could God use such a reprobate? This guy is a scoundrel! I don't know any other word to use to describe him. He cheated his brother, lied, and duped his blind father. He is certainly a strange person to receive a revelation from God. He is not a person with deep religious convictions. He is a fugitive with a deep need. Yet he has a dream—a vision—about God.

There ought to be some comfort in that fact for the rest of us. We are all scoundrels, sinners, in one way or the other, aren't we? This story reveals that you don't have to be a saint for God to appear to you. The marvel is that God came unexpectedly to Jacob in what appeared to be a God-forsaken place. He certainly didn't expect to find his God in this barren place. He probably assumed that his God was back in the home he had left, but he discovered that his God was there in this wilderness place as well.

God Often Appears in Unexpected Places and Ways

Others have also discovered that God comes unexpectedly and in strange places. God appeared in a burning bush to Moses on a mountainside while he was tending sheep. Jeremiah was taking a walk and he had a vision of God through a pot boiling on a fire and while watching a potter at work. Elijah fled after threats on his life from Queen Jezebel and hid in a cave depressed, isolated, lonely, and frustrated. In that isolated cave, he heard God in a still, small voice. Two men were walking west from Jerusalem toward Emmaus, when suddenly a stranger began to walk with them. They discovered later that this stranger was the resurrected Christ. Saul of Tarsus was traveling toward Damascus to persecute Christians when he met Christ, whom he had been persecuting. God sometimes comes into our lives in unexpected ways and in unexpected places.

After his dream of the angelic ladder, Jacob decided to set up a stone at Bethel to mark the place. "This is the gate of heaven. This is none other than the house of God." But out of Jacob's splendid vision came only a shallow commitment. Even in his desire to be blessed, Jacob was still the schemer and the supplanter. He attempted to bargain with God. "Okay, God. I will do what you want if . . . if you will bless me and you will take care of me and keep me safe."

He was still trying to scheme, even with God! This was not a devout prayer, but at least it was a beginning of faith. Yet even that vision faded. Jacob had a splendid vision of God, but it gradually became dim.

Jacob Arrives at Laban's Home

Jacob continued his journey over into Mesopotamia and finally arrived at the home of his uncle Laban. When he met Rachel, Laban's daughter, for the first time, he fell head over heels in love with her. He decided on the spot that she was the "woman I want to marry." When Jacob was welcomed by his uncle, Laban noticed his eagerness to marry his daughter. This over eagerness causes Jacob to fall into the same kind of trap that his brother Esau did when he had to have something to eat immediately. Just as Esau was willing to do anything for the bowl of lentil broth, Laban noted Jacob's insatiable desire for his daughter. Laban had observed that his nephew came to Haran alone, without a caravan or great riches and possessions. He came as a solitary figure. Laban was no fool, and he knew that this young man had likely fled from some problem back home. Maybe Jacob even told him the story.

Laban offered his nephew work and asked him to set his own wages. Rather than bargaining, Jacob promptly stated that he would work seven years for Rachel. That was a commitment far beyond the actual worth of a woman in the marriage "bargaining" of that day. Maybe he was paying what he thought she was worth to him. What he revealed was his willingness to pay any price for her. The seven years, the story states, were but "a few days" to Jacob.

On his wedding night Jacob was either too drunk or too utterly gullible, because Laban performed another act of deception by sending his older daughter Leah to the nuptial tent as Jacob's bride. Jacob didn't know until the next morning that he had married Leah instead of Rachel. Then he was furious. But Laban said, "Now wait a minute. She is the older of my daughters. Isn't the older given in marriage before the younger in your country? But I tell you what I will do. I'll let you marry Rachel if you will stay and work a while longer." In about a week Jacob married Rachel, and then he served Laban another seven years and then six more beyond that.

Jacob Schemes Again

There is a lot of Jewish humor in this story as it unfolds in the next section, and those of us who are removed from it by centuries have difficulty seeing it. But it is clearly there. Jacob is now depicted as contriving to get the upper hand on his trickster uncle. We saw earlier how Rebekah was a schemer. This approach to life must have run in their family, because Laban was the same way. But Laban didn't know that his nephew was even better at contrivance than he was. They made a deal so Jacob could have his own flock. Jacob said, "I'll just take the spotted sheep and goats and any lamb born black to finish my flock." Normally this would be only a small part of the flock. After they made this agreement, Laban immediately removed the spotted animals and black lambs from the flock. The Jewish listeners to this story would have laughed heartily at the crude, comical, and shrewd methods Jacob used to increase his flock.

In just a few years, Jacob grew exceedingly wealthy. He had huge flocks and decided to leave Laban and return home. Right before they left, Rachel stole the pagan gods of Laban. These were probably little wooden or stone idols. Laban pursued them and demanded his gods back. The use of humor continues in the story. Laban searched frantically through Jacob's tents and goods to find these gods while Rachel calmly sat on top of the little saddlebags where she had hidden them. She said, "I'm sorry I can't rise. The way of women is upon me." Through humor, the storyteller depicts the uselessness of these gods as a woman is sitting on them. Yet the God of Jacob protects him and guides his family toward home.

I want you to think about something else in this story. If it doesn't trouble you, it ought to. Sometimes we feel that we can simply open the Bible anywhere and find a moral lesson that will clearly direct us in how we ought to live and make our decisions. If you plan to look to this story for a clear moral teaching for your life, you will have trouble. Jacob represents a man who schemed and connived his way through life. He cheated his brother out of his inheritance, deceived his father, and manipulated and used his uncle to get his own way. Much of his life was spent in intrigue and scheming. You might expect me, as a preacher, to tell you that Jacob's lifestyle brought him to an awful end. But that is not the story. The story states that he was richly blessed. Through his plotting and conspiring, he ended up with large flocks and great possessions.

Goodness Is No Guarantee for Success or Prosperity

What is the truth of this story? It is simple. Look around you. There are many people in society who scheme, cheat, defraud, and deceive . . . and become wealthy. Sometimes they remain healthy into a ripe old age. Many of these people may even be atheists and never darken a church door. Just because a person is a Christian or committed to God is no guarantee that he or she will be healthy, wealthy, wise, or rich. The Jacobs of life often use the Esaus to reach their goals, and they may also manipulate the Isaacs. They don't care how you feel about what they do. They are only concerned with what it will all do for them. These people use others without giving it a second thought. Dishonesty and their quest for power and success cause these people to use others.

The Wrestling Match at Jabbok

We have finally come to the riverbank at Jabbok. Jacob's inner nature is the reason for this crucial encounter at midnight. Up to this point in Jacob's life, I have to be honest with you: I see nothing in his character to demonstrate that he is a person worthy of being followed anywhere. I like Esau a lot better. He is a much more likeable guy than Jacob. Jacob is a hard guy to like. If you were in business with him, you had better keep your eye on him. You'd know that he would try to manipulate you and the business to get his way. On the riverbank that dark night centuries ago, he has a strange encounter. He is all alone, and he wrestles with a stranger. Who is wrestling with him? I think part of his wrestling match is within himself. The next morning, he is to meet his brother Esau, whom he has not seen since he cheated him twenty years earlier. He has heard that Esau is coming to meet him with four hundred armed men. That is not a nice welcoming committee for a family reunion.

So what does Jacob do? He schemes first, as seems to be a part of his nature, then he prays. He decides that first he will send out his servant wives and their children at the front of the caravan. Next will follow Leah and her children, and last he will send Rachel and her children. Ahead of them he will send servants with a host of sheep, goats, camels, cows, and more as gifts for Esau to try to "bribe" him. Jacob hopes that these gifts will buy him forgiveness with his brother.

After he finishes scheming, he goes apart to think and pray. There in his tent all alone, he wrestles with God. He strives with this individual . . . angel . . . stranger . . . God. At times it seems he will win, and at other times it seems the stranger will win. As the day begins to break, this stranger says, "The dawn is coming, and I must leave." Why? Is this comment to be taken seriously? Or is it like the comment of Jesus on the Emmaus road when Luke wrote that it looked as though Jesus would go farther until the disciples asked him to stay?

Jacob and the angel have struggled all night. Suddenly Jacob realized the real strength of his opponent. It seems as if, with his finger, this angel suddenly touches Jacob's thigh and it is thrown out of place. Immediately Jacob becomes lame but continues to hang on to his opponent like a drowning man. He realizes that this opponent has never used all his strength before. As he hangs on Jacob cries, "Bless me before you leave." "What is your name?" the stranger/angel asks. Jacob replies, "I am supplanter, hanging on by the heel, trickster." "Now your name will be Israel," the angel responds, "one who wrestles with God, the rule of God. You will be the leader of a great nation."

From that encounter with the angel/Spirit of God, Jacob goes away limping. Blessing doesn't always bring health. This blessing makes Jacob a lame man. But even in his limping, he is a better man, a new man, a transformed man. At Jabbok, Jacob becomes Israel. In this meeting with God, he receives not a stolen blessing but the personal blessing of God on his life.

Our Jabbok

At this moment, where is your River Jabbok? Have you met God in some lonely hospital room as you sat by the bed of a sick child, husband, wife, daughter, or son? Have you wrestled with God in some low moment of defeat, failure, grief, disappointment, sin, or depression? Has there been some secret sin that has crushed your life down to the ground? Has there been some frustration, some agony that has caused you to go looking for things, possessions, or wealth? In any moment when you wrestle with God, hopefully you will find peace, love, joy, and a presence that sustains you. You can't get that through manipulation or by scheming. It is a gift from God. Have you found it? I hope so.

Esau: Exchanging Gifts

Genesis 25:24-34; 27:1-46; 33:1-4

Whether we realize it or not, much of life is spent "exchanging" things. We often see this in a material way after Christmas, when stores are busy with people exchanging some of the gifts that others spent so much time seeking to give them. There is a husband who wanted a fishing rod, but he got ski poles instead. There is a wife who wanted a blue dress, size eight, and her husband got her a green dress, size fourteen. There is a husband who wanted a Remington razor; his wife got a Schick straight razor instead of an electric. We could go on and on. Gifts are exchanged because of wrong sizes or colors, or sometimes people just don't like what they have received. For many, Christmas is the season of exchanging gifts.

One of the saddest kinds of exchanges, though, can be exchanging the higher values of life for the lesser values. Many give away the greater gift for the lesser gift. George Orwell wrote *1984* in 1949, and the date 1984 was supposed to be a time in the future in which the totalitarian forces would have taken over the world. In this dystopian novel, Orwell depicts a time when men and women have no real rights. They have given up their freedom in exchange for Big Brother to control the world. Everywhere you see the sign "Big Brother is Watching You!" One of the leading characters in this novel is Winston Smith. He works for the Ministry of Truth preparing Newspeak, a version of English that reworks all the past newspaper stories so they fit with the propaganda of the party ideology. He writes in such a way that nobody can understand what he is saying. In this way, he can make unorthodox opinions impossible to grasp.

While working for the government, Winston falls in love with Julia, a coworker. The Anti-Sex League has forbidden personal love, stressed the virtue of celibacy, condemned normal sexual love, and encouraged procreation by means of artificial insemination. Romantic love is supposed to be nonexistent and a heinous offense to the party. Winston also dares one day to criticize Big Brother. He is arrested and tortured. He is taken to the dreaded Room 101, where his worst fears have been deduced. When he is taken there, he is told,

> Things will happen to you from which you will not recover, if you live a thousand years. Never again will you be capable of ordinary human feeling. Everything will be dead inside you. Never again will you be capable of love, or friendship, or joy, or living, or laughter, or curiosity, or courage, or integrity. You will be hollow. We shall squeeze you empty, and then we shall fill you with ourselves.[1]

Winston loses his integrity when his greatest fear is realized as a rat in a cage is pushed toward his face. He cries out that this punishment should be inflicted on Julia and not on him. When he says that, the "thought police" know that his integrity is gone, and he will be a loyal party member now.

There are some parts of our world today where the totalitarian powers are almost like Orwell's projections. The government attempts to tell its people how to think and what to do. Most of us would say we don't have that kind of problem in our country, and yet some of us live out our lives in such automatic, routine, traditional ways that many of us are hollow men and women who have been filled with somebody else's purpose. We have exchanged our real freedom for lesser values and find our lives determined by advertising, clan behavior, and cliché images. Sometimes our political leaders, and even religious leaders, say and do things that make us question whether we are not closer to this kind of totalitarian control than we want to admit.

An Ancient Story

Let us look at two Old Testament characters whose story is centuries old. This ancient story gives us some insights about life itself, and so let's see if we can gather from this story some message for us as we reflect on the challenge of dealing with the many exchanges we face in our life's journey.

Twins were born to a family. The first child was named Esau, meaning red, which was likely due to his red hair. He grew up to be his father's favorite son because he was the hunter in the family. Jacob was the second-born son. He came from his mother's womb hanging on to the heel of his brother. He was his mother's favorite. Years went by and they grew up. The mother contrived ways that her favorite son, who was the second by birth, might in some way become the more prominent one. One day Esau came in from hunting tired and weary. It is not known how long he was gone on this hunting trip, but when he returned he found that his brother had cooked a red broth over the fire. The writer uses a lot of symbolism here in the Hebrew language. Esau pleaded with Jacob, "Give me something to eat. I am starving to death." The broth Jacob had prepared was not a red beef broth but was probably a lentil broth. Jacob wanted to make sure his brother did not clobber him later when he discovered his deception. And seeing this as an opportunity to take advantage of his brother, Jacob demanded, "Swear to me that you will give your birthright for it." His brother, who was too hungry to make a wise decision, agreed to give away his own birthright that he might have satisfaction in the moment.

A Sensory Response

To me, one of the interesting things in this story is the account of a man who is willing to give away his own birthright for the immediate satisfaction of his physical appetite. Down through history, many have responded to life like Esau. They have lived too much by their sensory impressions. Adam and Eve found that the fruit was appealing to the eye, and they gave up their Garden of Eden for it. Samson was attracted to a woman named Delilah and told her the secret of his power because of his love for her, and he lost his hair, his power, and his life. David yielded to his physical lust, committed adultery with Bathsheba, and lost his sense of close fellowship with God. Ahab, who already had great wealth, coveted a small garden that belonged to another man and killed so that his appetite might be satisfied, but then he came under the condemnation of God. For only thirty pieces of silver, Judas betrayed Christ. Too often, because of some response to our physical senses, we sell our own birthrights for physical satisfaction and lesser values.

Desiring Immediate Satisfaction

Notice also that Esau gave away his birthright because he wanted his desire satisfied immediately. He could not wait. One of the central points of the story historically is that Jacob is depicted as the one who has the power to wait. Although the writer honestly reveals the way Jacob tricked his brother, he also portrays Jacob as the one who can wait for the promises of God to be fulfilled. Esau, on the other hand, is revealed as one who cannot wait.

One of the tragedies of our lives is that often we cannot wait. We want what we want immediately. All kinds of ads try to seduce us into fulfilling our desires instantaneously. "Learn Spanish in thirty days." "Learn how to play the piano without any effort." "Learn how to become a star basketball player without practice." These messages are sent to us on how we can achieve certain things without struggle, discipline, or any kind of commitment. "Be a success overnight," some declare. "Rise to the top of the business." Too often we buy into this life philosophy because we want immediate satisfaction in the present moment. Sometimes we are too much like Esau, and we crave instant satisfaction for our desires. We are unable or unwilling to wait. But like a farmer who plants his seed in the ground and then waits for the crop to grow, we must learn to wait for the promises of the future to be realized.

Not Anticipating the Result of Our Decision

Do you think that if Esau had realized what he was giving up when he surrendered his birthright, he would have acted so quickly? He simply thought, "Oh, I am starving. What difference does anything else make at this moment?" Later he would reflect on what he had given up and realize that he released his double portion of the inheritance and his right to be the legal heir in charge of all the family affairs.

How quickly and easily we sometimes fall prey to our desires or needs of the moment and then later rethink the situation and wish we had not acted as we did. "Oh, if I had only known the consequences," we cry, "of course I would not have done what I did." If you and I could only see further down the road, we would acknowledge that we would not have taken a particular course of action. We must learn to anticipate the consequences of our thoughts and actions.

Several years ago, a ship hit a reef and began to sink. All the passengers were removed safely, and only the captain and the first mate remained aboard the ship. The captain was getting ready to get in the lifeboat and the first mate said, "I must go back and get my billfold." The captain cried, "Forget it, man! Come on now. We don't have time!" Thinking that the man had gotten in the boat with him, the captain shoved the boat off only to realize that the first mate had gone back aboard the ship to get his billfold. Suddenly the captain heard an awful gurgling sound as the ship was pulled down into the swirling vortex that carried it quickly beneath the surface. Later, when the first mate's body was found, he was clutching his purse. His billfold contained only a few small coins. Not for a moment would he have sacrificed his life for these few coins. But we have to understand that he never thought that he would die. And many of us never think for a moment, when temptations come upon us and we respond weakly and thoughtlessly by what we say or do, that consequences beyond our control will follow. If we knew it, of course, we would not do it. But a part of learning how to live authentically is having a sense of anticipation of what may happen as a result of what we set loose in our lives or in the lives of others. We must look ahead before we decide in the present.

Various Exchanges in Life

Think of the ways we make "exchanges" in our lives. Let us reflect on some things we need to heed and do. Let us be careful that we do not exchange today for tomorrow. A lot of us live in the tomorrows of life rather than today. We live for the time when we will finally finish high school or college, get out of the service, or retire. We live for the day when we will get married and buy a cabin by the lake or in the mountains or at the beach. We live for the time we will have a car or a second car. We always live off in the future. Little authentic living is happening in the present. We have exchanged the present for tomorrow and have not learned how to live authentically for today.

Let me also suggest that we do not exchange today for the past. We should not exchange what we can receive today for what has happened before this moment. Many live like that. We live on bygones. We live in the past when we were in high school on the football team, or playing tennis, or head cheerleader.

Sometimes we live in our past regrets. Scripture says that Jacob later pretended to be his brother and received Esau's blessing from their father. Because of this deception, he fled to save his life. Jacob could have lived out his life regretting that act, but he did not. He learned to live in the moment by finding a job, getting married, and later returning home. At the same time, Esau was also living his life in a normal way. When they met later, it was evident that they had both lived productive lives. Life went on despite their past.

Regretting Past Mistakes

But some of us cannot live in the present because we spend so much time regretting mistakes made in the past. We spend today in sorrow over some past sin, act, deed, or word. This prevents us from living effectively today. "My sin is ever before me," we say. We have not found forgiveness. Our guilt so overwhelms us that we cannot rise up as forgiven men and women and live effectively in the present. Our past is a huge burden that crushes us, and we are not able to function under its heavy load today.

Some of us carry the past with us in the way that we focus on past hurts, mistakes, or wrongs done to us. We reflect too much on what people have said that hurt us or offended us. We now spend our lives reacting to these deeds, thoughts, or actions, and we are controlled by the past. It is tragic indeed when something unfortunate has happened to us in the past and it still dominates our lives today. We let a past event or the behavior of another control our own behavior. There are people in the congregations I served as pastor who had somebody say something or do something to them in the past, maybe five, ten, or fifteen years ago, and they no longer speak to them today. That is not a Christian attitude. We need to find a sense of forgiveness and bury that past experience or sin. We need to go on and live in the present.

In his book *Habitation of Dragons*, Keith Miller writes about a time when he was in a discussion group, and each person in the group was sharing something from their childhood experience. When it was Alice's turn, she spoke hesitantly about her past. Alice indicated that she was brought up in an orphanage and longed to be adopted. Every time a family came to look her over, she tried so hard that she drove them away. She felt that she was not attractive, so people were not too eager to adopt her. Then one day a family came and wanted to take Alice home. She was so excited that she jumped up and down and began to cry. She was told by the head of the home that she had to remember this was only a trial. The family wanted to see whether she was a good fit. But Alice said she knew it would work out. Alice went to stay in the home and enjoyed life so much. She skipped off to school every day and her life was filled with great joy. But after several months, she came home from school one day and no one was there. She saw her suitcase with her coat thrown over it sitting in the hallway. It slowly dawned on her what this meant. "They didn't want me," she said. "And I hadn't even suspected." She paused for a moment and then continued, "That happened to me seven times before I was thirteen years old." Keith Miller said that he and others in the group began to cry for her and her tragic past. But then Alice said, "Don't; I needed my past. You see—it brought me to God."[2] Here is a woman who was not delighting in her past, but she learned from it and it opened a relationship for her with God.

The Future Is Not Necessarily Determined by Past Actions

One of the beautiful lessons in the story of Esau and Jacob is how Esau, who had been so angry with Jacob for stealing his blessing that he wanted to kill him, nevertheless, greeted his brother as he returned years later with love and an embrace (Gen 33:1-4). He did not let the past deception of his brother determine his attitude later. Don't let your past continue to destroy your life today because of something that may have happened in days gone by. Learning to feel the power of God in this moment can enable you to deal with the past and go on creatively to live in the present.

Some of us continue to cling to and lament over old grievances and old hurts. We let other people's behavior determine ours. We let other people's hatred, hostility, cruelty, or whatever it is make us hostile, cruel, and ugly. Do not respond with that kind of negative reaction. It is not Christlike. Do not let un-Christlike behavior determine what you become. Learn to be more like Christ and return good for evil, love for hatred, and hope for despair. That is the more Christlike way. Hold to his higher way. Quit playing the game of "If only I had not done this or had done something else," "If I had not married so and so," "If I had gone to this or that school." Let us end this chapter and go on to begin a new chapter of our lives with new print, new direction, and new meaning. Let's close the door to yesterday, open the door to tomorrow, and go forward with enthusiasm.

When we first moved to Louisville, we had a flowering cherry tree in the yard behind our dining room window. We enjoyed it in the springtime because the blossoms were so beautiful. We had a bird feeder in the tree, and we loved to watch the birds from the window. One year we noticed that something had happened to our favorite cherry tree. Unfortunately, it was dying. After it died, I began to wonder, "If I had called someone from the nursery sooner," or "If I had just fertilized it more," or "If I had just done this or that," would it have made any difference? But it was too late for the "if only" kind of discussion. Finally, I cut down the tree and saved whatever wood I could to burn in our fireplace. The rest I threw away. For me that tree became symbolic of how I needed to learn to face my past. There are some situations where we finally reach a point that we realize we cannot do anything more. We must draw from these experiences the best we can. Learn from them. Distill from them something that can help our lives now as little or as much as possible, but then go on. We must close that door and move toward the tomorrows ahead of us.

Live Meaningfully Today

Let me encourage you not to exchange today for the yesterday that was. Do not exchange today for the tomorrow that may be. Learn instead to live meaningfully today. This is the day that we have. We cannot undo the past. What has gone behind us is irreparable. We cannot undo it. It has been done. But what lies before us still has possibilities of being changed by what we may do in the present moment.

Emerson once said that Thoreau made an observation that he thought was so insightful: "As long as a man stands in his own way, everything seems to be in his way." Don't stand in your own way by holding on to old grudges, old mistakes, and old pains. Let them go. Live in the present. Find the power of Christ that can enable you to live. The exciting thing is that when Jacob later returned home to his family, his brother Esau did not meet him with hatred but met him instead with open arms, and they embraced. Jacob came back fearful because of what he had done. But his brother, whom Jacob had wronged, was the first to forgive him and embrace him.

There is a Latin phrase in one of Horace's odes, "Carpe diem," which means "seize the day." The image is of a teacher who grabs hold of a student's sleeve. Let's see if we cannot seize the day. This day is the gift we have. "This is the day that the Lord has made. I will rejoice and be glad in it." This day is God's gift to you and to me. This present moment. This hour. This day. Use it. Let God's spirit nourish your life and enrich it. I like what a ninety-three-year-old man said once. He realized that he could no longer live by himself and didn't want to live with his daughter, so he decided it was time for him to go live in a nursing home. He made a visit to a local nursing home, and the manager took him into a large room where older people were sitting staring into space. The man said, "Well, I'll tell you what. One thing's for sure; if I'm going to come to this place, we have got to turn this waiting room into a living room."

Let us be like this man and live in the present. This is the gift that God has given to us. No matter how dark the night, no matter how dreary the storm may appear in the darkness of midnight, remember that the morning always comes. And the morning reminds us that the God of the dawn has come in the risen Christ, who continues to guide our lives. Believe in the coming of the dawn. Dawn will come.

Accept the Future

When we learn to live in the present, that means we can accept the future. Esau made the decision to accept the future time he had with his brother, Jacob, and not focus on the past that was gone and could not be undone. Learning to accept the future enables us to live more realistically in the present that we have. Don't exchange the present for the past or the future. Learn to live in this moment. When we learn to live in the present, then we can live in anticipation of the future.

I read about a city called Flagstaff, Maine, where they constructed a dam near the town that was going to bury it under tons of water. What do you suppose happened to that town once the people knew that their homes would be buried under hundreds of feet of water? Nobody painted their homes anymore. Nobody made repairs. The whole town quickly went down in the dumps because everyone knew that soon it would not exist. As somebody observed, "When you have no faith in the future, there is no power in the present."

That was the kind of despair George Orwell was talking about in his novel. The people in *1984* saw no possibility in the future, so there was only despair for them. But you and I know there is a possibility in the future, because the future belongs to God. Hear what the writer in the small Epistle of John says: "God is love" (1 John 4:7-12). God is the source of love. He is the origin of love. He is the creator. And because God is a God of love, he has given us life. Life, then, originated out of God's gift of love. He gave us life, and out of his love for us he sustains us. Because God is the God of love, we can trust in the future. We commit the future to the God of love who cares for us, loves us, and has come to redeem us as we have seen it evidenced in Christ Jesus our Lord.

The word "January" comes from a Roman god named Janus. This two-faced god was supposed to be able to look to the past and the future at the same time. The God we have seen in Jesus Christ faces all directions at once. He is omnipresent—in all times and places. For Christians, the Gospel has assured us that we can look to the past knowing that the good God who created us was with us in our past. In the present, we have the God who sustains us, and we know we can look to the future with confidence that God will continue to undergird us with his presence. We can lean on him and trust him because we know that he is there and will always be there. If you and I are going to move from our current spot, we must begin at the place where we are. We must learn to live in the present and realize that God is with us in this moment. Don't exchange the present for the past or the future. Live in the present, which is God's gift to you now. The end of the year symbolically marks a time of concluding the past year and closing a chapter of our lives. At the beginning of a new year or today, live in the time you have now.

I spent several summers working in the mountains of Virginia at a Boy Scout camp. One of the things I enjoyed about that camp life was the rustic setting. We did not have electricity or other conveniences. Usually the counselor's campsite was far back from the main dining hall. We would always have a campfire at the end of each day. Then we would have to walk back into the darkness of the night toward our campsite. I didn't worry too much about that when I had a flashlight throwing a long beam in front of me. One of the things I learned quickly was that if I shone my light too far down the path and tried to see way down the pathway, I could not walk far. I learned to cast my light beam right in front of me, and as I walked in the path where I was shining the light, I was able to see and continue moving forward.

God has never fully told us what lies ahead of us in the future, except that he is there. As we see the light in the pathway before us, let us step into that light, and when we step into that light, more light goes before us to illumine our path, and more light will come. We live in the present with the assurance of the God who goes before us into the future. Don't exchange the greatest value you have—your birthright as a child of God—for your own strength and your own initiative. It is never sufficient. Step into the light of God. God's light provides the clearest guidance on how to live today, how to find forgiveness for yesterday, and how to live with assurance about tomorrow.

5

Joseph: Knowing Where You Are

Carlyle Marney, who served for a number of years as a pastor in North Carolina, told of an Irish setter that his family had. When the dog was about two years old, he was often picked up by strangers who thought he would make a great hunting dog. But Marney said they discovered after a short while that Old Red wasn't good for much, and they would set him free. He would always find his way back home. The dog was primarily a pet for the family's young girls.

The dog, Marney observed, knew only three things—where his food dish was, the rattle of keys, and the word "go." Whenever somebody said the word "go," the dog would come rushing to jump in the family car. The Irish setter, to quote Marney, liked "to sit up in the back seat just like a deacon, as if he were telling you where to go, here and there."[1] One day the dog was half asleep while Marney's wife was talking to a neighbor. "Well, I have to go now," she said. When she mentioned the word "go," the dog's ears shot up, and he jumped up and started racing across the floor. He hit the freshly waxed floor and swapped ends about four times, knocking over various pieces of porch furniture and breaking through the screen door—all because he heard the word "go." Dr. Marney said that this dog was busy outrunning himself!

That Irish setter has become symbolic to me of much of life today. We become so caught up in going somewhere in a rush that we are outrunning ourselves. Studies reveal that stress is one of the biggest problems that many people face in the workplace. One of the ways we have tried to deal with our need to rush is by speeding up everything else. We have developed instant breakfast, instant steaks, instant tea, instant coffee, smart phones with instant texting or emails, microwaves to make food ready to eat instantly. Many still read *Reader's Digest* so they don't have to read a whole novel, a technical book, or a magazine. Others get their news from Twitter, Facebook, or other social media. We can glance quickly at a digested version. Fast foods, microwave ovens, texts, and emails assist us in our ways of haste. Many of us find ourselves so busy trying to get somewhere that we spend all our time going and never discover where we are or who we are in the process.

If you ask a high school student, "What do you want to study in college?" many of them say, "Well, I . . . I don't know yet." This can still be true when they are a junior or sometimes even a senior in college. But young people, don't be discouraged. There are some fifty-year-old men and women who still don't know what they want to be when they grow up. They are still struggling to try to find out who they are and where they are in the process of living.

Bill Bradley, a noted basketball player of a few generations back, used to be able to hit a shot without even looking at the basket. A sports columnist asked him one day, "How can you hit that shot without looking where you are throwing the ball?" "You learn," he said, "to develop a sense of knowing where you are." That is a good observation not only for basketball but for all of life. If we are going to discover who we are, we must know where we are in life.

Joseph as a Model for Living

Joseph is our model in this chapter for discovering some lessons on knowing where we are. He is no ideal example of a person who had his life together. He is a flawed hero. The biblical record about Joseph covers chapters 37 through 50 in Genesis. This epic presents an account of Joseph's attempt to find himself. As a young man, he struggled to know where he was. The negative reaction of his brothers to his dreams about the whole family bowing down to him is not surprising. His superior attitude and favorite son position did not generate admiration or strengthen the family unity. His arrogance and conceit only created hatred and jealousy. He was a pampered young man whose colorful coat with its long sleeves depicted not a working man but the attire that was suitable for the leisure class. The rest of the family was engaged in hard manual labor while he assumed the role of a princely lord who had a favored position with his father. His self-conceited attitude indicates that he was still trying to discover who he was.

In the novel *Dr. Zhivago* by Boris Pasternak, there is a scene where Russian soldiers have arrested some insurrectionists. Among them is a young man named Terioshka Galuzin. He and several others are led to the edge of a ravine to be shot. As they are being lined up to be killed, Galuzin's nerves fail him and he pleads, "Forgive me, comrades, I'm sorry, I won't do it again, please let me off. Don't kill me. I haven't lived yet."[2]

Who among us cannot make that declaration? A young teenager who is struggling to know who he or she is exclaims, "I'm just beginning to live." As a young mother sees her new baby, she says, "I'm just beginning to live." Another says, "I'm just beginning college" or a new job, or have just retired. "I was married only last week." "My child is in the first grade." "I'm just now beginning to live!" When do we begin to live and discover where we are in this journey called life?

Joseph demonstrates that we don't discover where we are simply by having some information or facts about ourselves. He already told his brothers too frequently that he was the favorite son of his father. He was the firstborn son of Rachel and the dreamer of grandiose dreams. But that information was not sufficient to reveal the real Joseph.

Who Are We?

Who are you? You might tell us how much you weigh, how tall you are, what color eyes you have, what your work is, whether you are single or married, man or woman. But does that reveal who you are? Who is this I, me, you, they, he/she creature? Who are you? Information cannot suffice to reveal who we are. We know that is not enough. There are students in school who can learn all kinds of formulas in geometry or algebra but do not know what to do with these formulas. What good is that information if you do not know when or where to use it? A student may learn all kinds of historical dates and information from the past. They have a good mind to memorize facts, but they do not know what to do with the facts they have. Unless we learn to use the information and facts, what good are they?

Several years ago, a young man traveled through Arkansas trying to sell books on scientific agriculture to some of the farmers. He stopped an old farmer in the field one day and showed him the books. The farmer thumbed through them. "Well, what do you think?" the young man asked. "Don't you want to buy these books? These volumes can help you farm twice as well as you are doing." The old farmer looked up at him and said, "Heck, son, I don't farm half as good as I know now."

Most of us, when we are honest, know what to do. Getting more facts is not what we need to do. Our biggest problem is using correctly the facts we have. Simply having information or facts is not sufficient.

The Need for Inner Strength

If we are going to learn where we are, we need self-control. As Joseph matured through his hard lessons, his behavior indicates that he had inner strength. Joseph was made a slave in Potiphar's house. Under his management, the household prospered. Potiphar's wife tried to seduce Joseph, but he rejected her temptation and fled out of the house, leaving behind his outer garment. When you consider Joseph's circumstances, it would have appeared better for him if he had yielded to the sexual advances of Potiphar's wife. "Who does he think he is?" she may have thought. "Slaves don't have rights. They are property." Whatever their masters wanted, they were supposed to do. Joseph was a young man who knew the urges of the flesh, but he also had high moral standards. He executed self-control at a difficult moment in his life.

The Importance of Self-control

You and I will discover where we are as we exercise self-control. When we let everybody else manipulate and use us, our lives are out of control. Taking control of your life is one of the real discoveries in knowing where you are. We live in a society that seeks to manipulate us along life's journey. Television, movies, newspapers, the internet, and magazines constantly send us messages on what to wear, what to eat, where to go, what to buy, or where to vacation. These advertising signals try to direct our lives and determine the kinds of people we become. Many young people are the subject of these pressures at school, in their use of leisure time, and in everything else they do. These external forces try to tell them who they are, what they can become, and what makes the "good" life. To be a mature person, every individual has to develop self-control.

I know a couple who wanted to raise their child free of all discipline. Whatever the child wanted to do, they gave her absolute freedom to do it. They said they didn't want the child to grow up with any feelings of inhibition. Well, this child is definitely growing up that way. What is she like? A brat! She spits water on people when they come on the porch, kicks them, knocks things off the table, and pays no attention to what anyone says to her. She does anything she wants, anytime she wants. Can you imagine what is going to happen to that child when she gets in school and her peers react to her when her parents are not around?

If a child is left free to think that he or she can act without any restraints, that child will have difficulty adjusting in society. Somebody else will build fences for her. One of the early lessons in life is learning how to live within some of the fences society sets and morality dictates. We have to learn to live within certain moral and behavioral boundaries if we are going to be a part of normal human society.

Self-control is an important factor in becoming an authentic person. A Quaker was accosted one day by a newspaper boy who was rude to him because he wouldn't buy a paper. As he walked away, a friend with him observed, "Why didn't you respond forcefully to this young boy who was so rude to you?" The Quaker replied, "Why should I let the behavior of that boy decide how I will act?" That is a difficult lesson to learn. Too often we simply respond in kind to the behavior of others. We only react. We allow others to control us. Those who have discovered where they are have learned the value of self-control. Our Lord is the prime example of self-control. He had all the resources of the universe at his disposal, but he chose the way of a servant. Christian self-control is living out our lives under the power of Christ, who has called us to a higher way of living. Rather than being controlled by situations and people around us, we rely on the inner strength of Christ's presence to determine our behavior.

A Sense of Inner Peace

Move further into the story of Joseph and you will find that he not only demonstrated self-control but also seemed to have an inner peace and a sense of being in tune with God. Even when he was sold into slavery, put in prison, and seemingly rejected at every turn, he seemed to be at peace with himself and sought to make the best of the situation. The way Joseph advanced in Potiphar's house shows him making the best of where he was. The Scriptures say that Potiphar's house was blessed because of Joseph. And he did the best he could even in prison.

Many times, all we do is spend our lives kicking against the sides of the universe when everything doesn't go our way. We want to roll up our tent, whine, shout angrily at God, and move on because we are not getting what we want. Joseph's inner peace came from an awareness that God was directing his life. Even when his life was difficult, he believed that God was present to sustain him. Later when Joseph rose to a position of great power in Egypt, he gave God the credit for all that had happened. God was working in his life during times of affliction as well as in times of prosperity.

Years ago, I heard about two pictures that were painted for a special celebration to emphasize peace. When the curtains were pulled back and the audience looked at the paintings, they saw that first one depicted a scene of pastoral serenity. A family was sitting down at a table for a country meal. In the background cows were grazing in the field. The family was bowing their heads in prayer.

It was a tranquil image of peace. When the curtain was pulled back on the second painting, they were startled by the force of the image of a mighty, rushing waterfall. The painting was so shocking at first that the viewers stepped back. They wondered what it had to do with peace until they noticed a limb jutting out from behind the waterfall. On this limb there was a bird's nest. In the nest a bird was singing to its heart's content. After the viewers reflected on the image for a moment, the symbolism became apparent to them. In the midst of the turmoil and storms around the bird's nest, within it was tranquility and peace.

This is the real Christian image of peace. It is symbolic of the peace Christ gives us. God doesn't remove all problems and difficulties from our lives, but he remains with us during these struggles and gives us his peace. "My peace," Jesus says, "I give to you."

Difficulties Are a Part of Life

Joseph also discovered that difficulties and problems are a part of life. Here was a young man who had been the favorite son of his father. He had his every need met. He thought he was the center of the world. His brothers became jealous and plotted at first to kill him, but they decided instead to sell him into slavery. Things went from bad to worse, for the household slave was soon cast into prison. His circumstances seemed to have reached the bottom. But amid all the difficulties, Joseph continued to have faith in God. He was certain that God's purpose for his life would triumph.

God has not promised us that life will be free of difficulties and problems. One of the worst lessons we can try to teach our children is that they should win at everything they do. Failure is a part of life. Everyone will experience failure, problems, or difficulties. Sometimes life is hard. We must learn to face this reality.

Several years ago, on the *Today Show*, a professor from MIT described a course he taught on failure. "Our society is oriented too much toward success," he said. "We have to teach young people and others that sometimes they will fail at what they do. They have to learn how to handle their failures." The announcer inquired, "Well, did anybody fail your course?" The professor said, "No, but I had two incompletes." Our path in life is filled with failures and incompletes. But amid our difficulties or failures, the presence of God is still with us. Failure or difficulties do not separate us from his sustaining grace.

When I was a young boy, I wanted to learn how to ride a bicycle. My sister had a bicycle, but she wouldn't let me ride it. One day when she wasn't around, I got on her bicycle and started riding it. I climbed on at a level spot, but then there was a long hill that reached a dead end where a fence was built at the edge of a small cliff, with railroad tracks at the bottom of the hill. I got on the bicycle and did a good job of balancing myself. Suddenly, I started down the hill. As I picked up speed, some folks on the side of the street began to yell, "Put on the brakes." But I didn't know how to put on the brakes. This was a bicycle with pedal brakes. The shouts grew louder as I continued going faster down the hill. "Put on the brakes, put on the brakes." I was so determined to prove I could ride that bicycle that I didn't take time to learn how to ride it properly. Fortunately, I ran into a parked car on the side of the hill, which brought me to a quick stop. I was lucky and only received a bloody nose. That was fortunate when you consider what might have happened.

Sustained by God's Presence

Often in life we will find ourselves failing in some way or another. We may not know how to put the brakes on or to avoid danger. Sometimes we will fail and may get hurt. Hopefully, we can learn from our failures and difficulties and become better people because of the lessons we learn. Joseph learned that during his difficulties and problems—even slavery and imprisonment—God was with him. Joseph was assured that God was in control. He believed in the providence of God. "You meant evil against me," Joseph later said to his brothers, "but God meant it for good, to bring it about that many people should be kept alive, as they are today" (Gen 50:20). He acknowledged God's presence in the bad as well as the good. God doesn't deliberately send evil, suffering, pain, and failure in our lives. But as Paul reminds us, "God can work in all things to bring about good" (Rom 8:28).

Joseph, who had experienced so much abuse at the hands of his brothers, developed into a forgiving person. His brothers had plotted to put him to death and then decided to sell him as a slave, and he was taken in chains to Egypt. In Egypt he rose to prominence in Potiphar's house as a slave, and then he became Pharaoh's right-hand man as the minister of agriculture. Later his brothers came down from Canaan during a famine in their country and sought to buy food from him. What did Joseph do? Did he take vengeance on them? No. Through a test in which he put his silver cup in Benjamin's sack, he discovered that Judah and the other brothers had also changed and were willing to remain as slaves rather than see their brother Benjamin enslaved. Joseph revealed who he was to his brothers and forgave them for what they had done twenty years in the past.

In times of difficulty, hurt, and abuse from others, one of the great lessons of a mature person is their willingness to forgive. To nurse old hurts, to cling to pains from the past, or to harbor old grudges is to deny the forgiving grace of God. This was certainly not an easy lesson for Joseph, but he gave evidence of a generous spirit.

God Goes Before Us

Finally, one of the great truths in the story about Joseph is that God was always going before him. Whether he was a slave or in prison, he trusted God. He didn't spend all his time looking back to Canaan where his family was and where everything had been ideal for him. He could have spent all his time thinking about "how wonderful life was back then." Instead, he focused on where he was now and looked to the reality of God's presence to sustain him. He trusted God to go before him into the future. In quiet trust, he leaned on God for assurance.

One day I was driving down a street and saw a church sign that read, "Don't be afraid. God has already gone ahead of you into the future." That is a good thought to remember. Whatever difficulties or problems you have, be assured that God has already gone ahead of you to be present for you. One of the sad notes in the story about the rich young ruler is that he came to Jesus seeking to discover where he was in relationship to God, but he was unwilling to accept the lesson he sought. In a painting by William Frederick about the rich young ruler, Jesus is depicted standing by the young man with his hand on his shoulder, pointing off into the distance. The commentary on this story is that the rich young ruler walks away sadly. He is unwilling to follow the instruction of Jesus.

Jesus has called us to come follow him into the future. He offers to lead us. When we follow him, we will surely know where we are.

6

Moses: Responding to God Is Charged with Responsibility

Exodus 3:1-8, 13-16

Like an ancient Egyptian pyramid, Moses towers over other figures in the Old Testament. He was the first great leader of the Hebrew people. He was the first and probably the greatest of the Hebrew prophets. His superior military leadership guided the Hebrew nation out of Egypt in their exodus as they escaped from bondage and as they traveled through the wilderness toward the promised land. Moses was also the great lawgiver as evidenced in the Ten Commandments. Under Moses' leadership the Hebrew tabernacle and the ark of the covenant were constructed. These were a part of Moses' contribution to Israel's history.

God's Providence in Moses' Life

Let us begin our study of Moses by noting the providence of God in his life. It seems that from the time of Moses' birth and throughout his life, God's hand was continuously guiding him. The biblical writer informs his readers that "a Pharaoh arose who knew not Joseph." The Israelites had been in Egypt four hundred years when Moses was born. During this time, they had slipped from a place of recognition under Joseph to being slaves. Pharaoh was afraid that the Hebrews would soon be too numerous to control, so he issued an edict to kill their children as soon as they were born. Hebrew parents, of course, tried to hide their children from Pharaoh's soldiers. When Moses was born, his parents hid him. They heard that the soldiers were looking to kill newborn babies, and Moses' parents thought of a way to hide their three-month-old baby boy. Many people learn this familiar story as children in Sunday school. Moses' mother constructed a small basket made from bulrushes and daubed it with tar and pitch to make it watertight, so it could float. Moses was put in this basket and hidden in the reeds near the riverbank where his sister could watch.

One day the daughter of Pharaoh came down to the river to bathe. She saw the basket in the reeds and probably heard the baby crying. The princess sent her maids to get the basket, and when she saw the child she knew he was a Hebrew baby but fell in love with this young infant and had pity on him. Immediately the sister of Moses, Miriam, rushed forward and said, "I know a good Hebrew nurse who can take care of this baby." The nurse, of course, was the mother of Moses. While Moses was in Pharaoh's palace, his own mother nursed him and taught him the Hebrew tradition and way of life. During the same time, according to this saga, Moses received nurture, training, benefits, and guidance in the Egyptian royal household from his adopted mother.

Moses spent forty years being trained both in the Egyptian and Hebrew ways of life. I am not sure exactly how age was determined then. A year may not have been measured exactly like we measure it today. One day Moses witnessed an Egyptian beating a Hebrew slave unmercifully. Moses killed the Egyptian man who was beating the slave. Moses probably thought that he would win the admiration of the Hebrew people with this act, but that did not happen. He fled for his life into the desert and ended up in Midian.

At Midian, Moses rescued the four daughters of Jethro from the harassment of some hostile shepherds when they came to water their sheep one day. Later Moses married one of Jethro's daughters, Zipporah, and then disappeared into the desert wilderness as a shepherd for forty years. This is the second forty years of his life. During this period of forty years, Moses learned the ways of the desert. As a shepherd, he learned not only how to care for sheep but also how one survives in that kind of climate and country. These forty years were preparing him for the next episode in his life.

After his burning bush experience with God, Moses confronted Pharaoh with the words from God: "Let my people go." After much difficult struggle and fierce plagues, the Hebrew people were freed. They crossed the Red Sea (Sea of Reeds)[1] and begin their wilderness wandering for forty years. During this time, the Hebrew people received the Ten Commandments, and Moses continued to guide them toward the promised land. Because Moses himself was disobedient to God, he was not allowed to go in. He was only allowed to ascend to the top of Mt. Nebo and look over into the promised land (Deut 34:1-4). Shortly afterward, he died and was buried at Moab at the age of 120. The saga of his life is divided into three distinct periods: forty years in the Egyptian palace, forty years as a shepherd, and forty years as the leader of the Hebrew people in the wilderness. The writer denotes clearly that God was directing, guiding, and using Moses throughout these years. Whatever else one wants to say about this story, there is no question that the writer indicates that God's providential hand was directing the life and path of Moses.

Difficult Choices for Moses

Moses faced difficult choices in his life. At some point, and we are not sure exactly when or where it was or what the circumstances might have been, Moses had to face the choice of whether he would keep the riches of Egypt or identify with the suffering of his own Hebrew people. Some writers have depicted this time of decision in Moses' life as though it came at a particular moment when he stood before the throne of Pharaoh. In this scene, Moses is pictured standing before his adopted mother, the daughter of Pharaoh and the princess of the royal court. Pharaoh states that he has now become old and it is time for his successor to be chosen. "Although you are not an Egyptian," Pharaoh says, "you are my adopted son. If you will choose my people and deny your Hebrew tradition, I will pass on to you my throne and you will become the next pharaoh." "No," Moses thunders, "I cannot do that!"

That is probably not the way it happened, but at some point and in some way, Moses did make a choice. His choice likely came at the moment in his life when he had to choose whether he would simply stand on the sidelines and remain an Egyptian, although he was a Hebrew, or whether he would become involved in the suffering of his Hebrew people. The first step of Moses' deliberate involvement and the point of his separation from the royal household came when he killed the Egyptian who was beating the Hebrew slave. He chose at that moment to become involved. He may have thought that his blow was justified and might be the spark to begin the revolution for his people's freedom, causing them to rally around him as their leader. But they didn't. The Hebrews said to him in essence, "Who are you? Why should we follow you?"

Moses took his stand to identify with his Hebrew kinspeople. But his action did not force them to choose freedom and follow him as their leader. He chose sides, but the Hebrew people would wait forty years before they got involved in their own freedom. The exodus would not begin with this one blow. An enslaved people would be slow to respond to the rallying cry of freedom.

The writer of the book of Hebrews, in his great catalogue of faithful people, penned, "By faith Moses, when he grew up, refused to be called the son of Pharaoh's daughter, preferring to suffer hardship with the people of God rather than enjoy the transient pleasures of sin. He considered the stigma that rests on God's Anointed greater wealth than the treasures of Egypt, for his eyes were fixed upon the coming day of recompense" (Heb 11:24-26).

Moses was willing to give up the security he knew in Egypt to venture into the unknown. But this was a costly decision. He rejected the security of the royal household. Could he have one day been a pharaoh? Who knows? If he refused to obey God, would there have been a tomb to Moses the pharaoh? We don't know. But one thing is certain. Instead of choosing the throne, he chose the way of tragedy, suffering, and pain. Rather than having a ruling scepter in his hand, he had a shepherd's rod. Rather than great wealth and power, he faced difficulties and struggles of wilderness wandering and the chastisement of the wrath of Pharaoh upon his life. It was a sharp descent from the palace to the desert. Moses was willing to make difficult choices to follow the leadership of God.

The Burning Bush Call of Moses

The call of Moses into God's service on Mt. Horeb is a strange but well-known story. Moses led his sheep up the mountain of Horeb or Sinai where he had gone numerous times before. He called this place "the mountain of God." While he was on Horeb one day, a day like other days I am certain, he saw a bush that was burning but not consumed by the flames. He knew a shrub like that should have burned quickly and turned to ashes. But for some reason the bush was not consumed. How was this possible?

How are we to interpret this story? Scholars have had all kinds of difficulty trying to explain the burning bush that was not consumed. Some have said that this shrub was like the "burning bushes" some of us have in our yards. In the fall of the year, the leaves on the burning bush turn bright red like fire. We had two burning bushes like that in our yard when we lived in Louisville, Kentucky. But I cannot believe that is the answer. Moses saw those bushes all the time. Why would this one's fall glow have captured his eye and made him think it was aflame?

Others feel strongly that this account should be taken literally; that it is evidence of the supernatural power of God. Still others believe it was an inner experience of Moses. These people have suggested that if you or I had been present with Moses, we would not have seen the burning bush. What happened was visible only within Moses' own consciousness. This vision addressed his mind alone in the same way that Jesus heard the voice of his Father say, "This is my beloved son in whom I am well pleased." Others around Jesus did not hear the voice but only heard thunder. Paul experienced a blinding light on the Damascus Road and saw and heard the risen Christ. But others on the same road did not see the light.

Whatever happened on the mountainside at Sinai was so vivid to Moses that it changed his life forever. The how is not important. The burning bush was the means of communicating God's presence to Moses. Moses saw within the bush that was not consumed the very presence of God. When the Exodus writer says that "the angel of the LORD appeared to him," this is a reference to the presence of God. Here in a thorn bush, on a mountainside of Sinai, God appeared to Moses. His experience was vivid and real in the sight and sounds he perceived within his own consciousness.

Fire as a Divine Symbol

Fire is often used as a divine symbol in the Scriptures. Abraham saw God in a blazing furnace of fire as he was called to follow God's direction to a city without foundation. A pillar of fire was the symbol of God's presence as he led the children of Israel through their wilderness wandering. John the Baptist proclaimed that the "one who comes after me will baptize you with the Holy Spirit and with fire" (Matt 3:11). Jesus said, "I have come to cast fire on the earth" (Luke 12:46). At Pentecost, tongues of fire came upon the disciples, symbolizing the coming of the Holy Spirit (Acts 2:1-3). The writer of Hebrews wrote that "our God is a consuming fire" (Heb 12:29). The symbolism of God as fire or flames has been vivid and real to many down through the ages. It is a symbolic way of speaking about the presence of God.

Whatever way Moses experienced the presence of God in that burning bush, it was a transforming encounter. His life was forever different. He experienced God intensely in the burning bush, and his life took a different direction. Why was Moses able to respond to God on that mountainside? I think he still had a sense of expectancy. I believe he was the kind of person who had learned, on mountainsides and in desert places, to be open to God. Elizabeth Browning wrote in *Aurora Leigh*,

> Earth's crammed with heaven
> And every common bush afire with God
> But only he who sees, takes off his shoes.

Moses was one who took off his shoes.

Moses' Sense of Expectancy

Moses was able to see and hear, so he responded when God addressed him out of a bush on a desert mountain. His sense of expectancy was vivid. Too often you and I don't see God anywhere. We can't even see God in church! God is everywhere, but our senses are so dulled that we can't perceive him. We simply do not know that God is constantly trying to make God's presence known to us.

The Response of Moses

Moses was not only open but was also responsive. He responded to the vision he had and stopped doing what he was doing. The writer notes that Moses said, "I will turn aside and see this sight." Curiosity first drew him to see this strange phenomenon. God can't get our attention sometimes because many of us never pause and stop to listen and see. We are always going, in a rush, so busy. I love the old saying that turns our expression upside down: "Stop doing what you are doing and just stand there!" We are often so busy going and doing that God can't get our attention.

But Moses turned aside and responded to God. Moses saw and heard God and responded in awe and reverence. As he approached the great mystery of the presence of God in the burning bush, he heard the voice say to him, "Take off your shoes, because you are on holy ground." He knelt in wonder, worship, and awe before God, who identified himself: "I am the God of your forefathers, the God of Abraham, the God of Isaac, the God of Jacob."

God revealed that he is a God of concern. God has "seen," "heard," and "knows" the misery, suffering, and plight of "my people. . . . And I have come down to rescue them." Granted, this is anthropomorphic language, but it indicates in clear imagery that God is not detached, abstract, remote, or indifferent to the sufferings of his people. He is a God who is so concerned that he "comes near." He tells Moses that he has come down to deliver the people and set them free.

Moses' Commission

Following his experience with God, Moses is commissioned. Whenever a person encounters God, he or she is also commissioned into service. God doesn't confront us with his presence simply to satisfy our needs. Out of our meeting with God, we are called into ministry for God. But Moses immediately protests: "Oh, God, who am I?" He is a reluctant prophet. "Who am I, God, to undertake such a task? I am a nobody. Who am I?" But God insists that he has chosen Moses to be his prophet. "I will be with you," God promises him.

I AM WHO I AM

Next Moses asks, "Who are you? Who are you, God? Who am I supposed to say is sending me?" God's response to this has kept scholars wrestling for ages to determine its precise meaning. The divine name in Hebrew is "Yahweh." The Hebrew phrase is usually translated, "I AM WHO I AM." Welling up in that phrase, Moses hears the explanation of the name of God. "Tell them that the One who has no beginning or end, whose existence is in the now, is the God who is sending you. Tell them that the God before whom you kneel in mystery and awe, the God of your fathers, the God who is not confined to this mountain, but the God who will lead his people out of slavery into the promised land, the God who is offended by injustice, will send his prophets to speak out against this oppression and set his people free. I AM WHO I AM," says God.

You and I have to define our existence by stating that we are the son or daughter of our parents. We are the product of our environment. We have been derived from what has gone before us. But God is "I AM WHO I AM." He is the eternal One without beginning or end. God is original, primary, absolute, and underived. He is the One who spends himself but is never exhausted, burns continuously but is not consumed.

"But God, they won't believe me," Moses continues to protest. "They didn't believe me when I killed the Egyptian to help them. They wouldn't follow me then. Also, Lord, I am not an eloquent man." Finally, Moses says, "Oh Lord, just send anybody else. Who am I?" At this point God becomes angry. "You are the one that I have chosen. Your brother Aaron can help you speak. You are the one who is to go. He will be your mouthpiece. Take your staff to work the signs."

A Reluctant Leader

Moses was a reluctant hero. He had a genuine sense of humility. But finally, he surrendered and followed God. How different he was from some brass preachers today who claim to have a special handle on God that gives them insights into every realm of truth. They rush into areas of theological thought with such absolute certainty where angels would fear to tread. The Exodus writer is careful not to put the primary emphasis on Moses but on God. As Martin Buber notes, "the glorification is dedicated solely to the God who brings about the events."[2]

As Moses reluctantly agrees to follow God, he is given three signs to assure him of God's presence with him: the staff becoming a snake, the leprous hand, and water changing into blood. Regarding the shepherd's staff or rod, God asks, "What is in your hand? Cast it on the ground." And Moses' staff becomes a snake. When Moses picks it up by the tail, it turns back into a staff again. His shepherd's rod is a sign of God's presence with him. Did Moses engage in a struggle of power with Pharaoh's magicians in Egypt? Snakes were often used as a part of Egyptian magic in Moses' day. Through various plagues that God sent upon the Egyptians, Moses demonstrated that God's power was superior to Pharaoh's magicians.

What's in Your Hand?

"Moses, what's in your hand?"

I want to ask you, "What's in your hand?" Others have been asked that question. "David, what's in your hand? You have only a few stones and a slingshot as you go out to confront a giant of a man. How can you do anything?" What's in his hand represents the power of God. "Elijah, what's in your hands? It's only a few sticks of wood that you are piling on an altar. What is that compared to the power of the high priests of Baal?" Yet the fire of God consumed Elijah's offering and revealed that God was in his hand. "Paul, what's in your hand? You have some thread and needles to mend tents." "Jesus, what's in your hand? It's only a cup and bread."

What's in your hands? Your hands may be gnarled from hard physical labor. Your hands may express the tender touch of a nurse. They may be the guiding hands of a teacher. They may be the confident hands of a surgeon, the trained hands of an athlete, the gentle hands of a parent, the gritty hands of a coal miner, the soiled hands of a farmer, the serving hands of a secretary, community worker, or minister, the experienced hands of a professional man or woman. What's in your hands?

Albrecht Durer was one of a family of eighteen children who lived in Nuremberg, Germany. He and a close friend named Franz Krigstein wanted to become artists. They made an agreement that Franz would work a while at manual labor so Durer could study and paint. Later Durer would work in order for Krigstein to have the same opportunity. Years passed and Durer became famous as an artist. But manual labor caused the hands of Franz to become gnarled and knotty. He realized that his stiff and knotted hands would not let him be the artist he had dreamed of becoming. He became deeply depressed.

One day Durer noticed his friend's hands as they were folded in prayer. "I can never give back the lost skills to those hands, but I can show my feeling of love and gratitude by painting his hands as they are now, folded in prayer, to show my appreciation of a noble and unselfish character." Swiftly he sketched the gnarled hands of his friend at prayer. That painting of his friend's knotty hands, gnarled by years of physical work, lifted up in prayer, have inspired countless people through the years.

What's in your hands, whatever kind of hands they are? God may not commission you to go into Egypt or to confront a pharaoh, but he will commission you to use your hands in his service. Let us hear the voice of God out of the "burning bushes" around us as he challenges each of us to respond to his call to go serve in his name.

7

Caleb: Overcoming Negative Vision

Numbers 13:1-33

In life there are two basic ways of seeing. One is positive, the other negative. One perspective sees only the darkness; the other can see the beginning of dawn. The one is able to see only defeat; the other is able to see victory. One is only able to see despondency; the other is able to see hope. One is able to see only a pile of rubble; another sees materials from which to begin rebuilding. One sees a dead-end street; another sees an opportunity to make a new road. One person sees a glass half empty; the other sees it half full. How do you see? Do you have negative or positive vision in life? Most of the time, when we talk with someone, we can tell rather quickly how they see. They reveal almost immediately in their conversation whether they see life with negative or positive vision.

Negative or Positive Vision

The biblical story about an obscure Old Testament figure named Caleb, one of the spies Moses sent to explore Canaan or what came to be called the "promised land," addresses our perspective about negative and positive vision. Let us look at this story for a moment. Notice, first of all, that some of the characters project a great deal of negative vision toward life. The children of Israel, according to this Old Testament selection, had moved to the edge of the promised land. They had traveled for forty years in the wilderness. Now Moses sent some spies to go into the land that lay before them to see what it was like. Twelve men, one from each tribe, traveled for forty days through the land, probably moving in the darkness of night and scurrying about here and there in the daytime, trying not to be seen, as they observed the land and the people who lived there. They discovered that, compared to the desert where they had been for forty years, this was a fertile land. It was indeed flowing with milk and honey. Their report pictured the land as fantastically rich with promise. To prove their point, they returned with pomegranates, figs, and a large bunch of grapes swinging on a long pole. All could see the great luxury of the land. Caleb was the spokesman. He declared, "Let us go up at once and occupy the country; we are well able to conquer it." Joshua sided with him, but the other ten were reluctant and exclaimed, "Wait a minute. These people look like giants to us." They were the sons of Anak, the "long-necked ones." Goliath, some scholars believe, may have been a descendant of this tribe.

A Grasshopper View

The men in the promised land looked gigantic to these former slaves. "We look like grasshoppers to them," they cried. Their attitude is astounding. God's presence had been with them through all their time in the desert, and now, as they got ready to enter the promised land, they took a tremendously negative view. Fear had overtaken them, and their enemy seemed like large giants. "We are grasshoppers," they said. Grasshoppers are helpless, feeble, and have a low perspective on life.

We all know something about the grasshopper view of life, don't we? Some of us, if we are older, can recall the days when we were small and everybody looked like giants to us. Remember the days in elementary school when you looked up at all the giants around you until you yourself began to grow up and you became a giant to someone else. It is amazing how often in life we see whatever obstacles arise before us as giants to be conquered. We feel as insignificant as grasshoppers, and a negative view slowly begins to permeate everything we do in our reaction to life. Instead of the highest goal possible, we reach toward the lowest maximum we can achieve as we seek to make our contribution in life. With this negative view, we try to get by with the least that we can. We often do this in our marriages. We do it in our church lives and in our business lives. We take this approach in almost every area of our lives. We aim at the lowest common denominator and live out our negative view. We become satisfied with the least we can do and do not reach for the highest potential within us.

Professors and teachers in school detect this perspective from students rather quickly. When they assign a paper to students, hands go up and a student asks, "Does it have to be ten pages? Can it be less?" Many students would not dream of writing a paper longer than the minimum number of pages. "Does it have to have a bibliography?" "Does it need footnotes?" Most of them want these extras left off so they can do the least amount of work required. Many do not have the desire to do the kind of research that will make them the best-informed students they need to be but seek, instead, the avenue that requires the least amount of effort. There is no excitement or enthusiasm for the subject. Too often that is the same approach we take toward our religion. It is our approach toward marriage, toward parenting, and, unfortunately, toward too much of life. The desire to get by with the least we can do is a negative attitude that is reflected in our words and deeds.

Charlie Brown came walking out of his house to feed Snoopy one day. Snoopy was lying on top of his doghouse. Charlie Brown said to him, as he poured his dog food, "This food has been no trouble at all for me to fix for you today. It is just dry cereal and all I had to do was pour some water in it and it is ready to eat." Snoopy looked at it, and after Charlie Brown walked away he thought, "I'd rather be worth a little trouble." The things in life that are worthwhile usually require a little trouble. But too often we give way to the negative view and not the positive, and we seek to do the least we can.

Losing Our Vision of God

Second, notice in these stories that the people had lost their vision of the power of God. The view of the other spies reflected a denial of God (Yahweh) and his presence with them (Num 14:9). In some ways it is almost astounding that this would happen to the children of Israel when they had lived daily with God going before them as a pillar of fire. Through this pillar of fire, God's presence was made known. Now, as they were finally getting ready to go into the promised land, the people of God had forgotten about his presence and saw only the giants looming before them.

A New Testament Illustration

Let us look briefly at a New Testament story that illustrates this point (Matt 17:14-20). Jesus has been transfigured before some of his disciples. Moses and Elijah appeared there on the mountain with Jesus. When Jesus came back down from the mountain following the transfiguration, he found a young youth who was possessed by a demon. He discovered that his disciples were unable to cure the boy, and he said, "Oh you of little faith." Sometimes we have lots of faith on the mountaintops of life, but when we come down into the valleys where there are difficulties and problems, our faith seems inadequate to sustain us.

Raphael, in a marvelous painting of this scene, shows Jesus on the mountaintop transfigured with Moses and Elijah. The disciples with him are lying on the ground in an attitude of deepest awe. Down in the valley below, the other disciples are surrounded by a crowd of people, with the father and his young tormented son whom the disciples are helpless to cure. Some are pointing up toward the mountaintop where Christ is and from whom they will draw their source of strength.

Fear of the New Challenge Before Us

Why do you suppose the Israelites and the disciples responded in such a negative way? For one thing, they were simply afraid. The Israelites saw the giants in the promised land, and they were fearful of confronting them. The giants seemed too formidable. We, too, know something of these kinds of fears when we seek to move forward in life. We see individuals who are too threatening to us. Danger seems to lurk around every corner. The obstacles appear too difficult, so we fall back in great fear. We can't face the challenge. It seems impossible.

The Israelites and disciples felt helpless, and we often do as well. We often have the "grasshopper mentality." We think that the giants in the land are going to destroy us as we meet them. All kinds of giants loom before us, and we feel helpless before their power. What can we do against the might of the world's powers when we feel so small and insignificant? We feel helpless because we forget the power of God. We think only about our own strength. We forget the strength that we draw from God. The Israelites and the disciples needed to realize that by themselves they were helpless, but as they drew upon the strength and power of God, he enabled them to meet whatever force lay ahead of them. And so can we.

Selfishness Stifles Us

Selfishness sometimes clouds our vision and causes us to lose sight of the power of God. We focus only on our own needs. What I do is for my comfort. What I do is for my convenience. Our chief concern becomes what is good for me and makes me healthy and wealthy. Only what satisfies me becomes my chief emphasis. We soon forget about the concerns and needs of others in society and look only at ourselves.

A psychiatrist advised a woman one day to remove a mirror over her kitchen sink and to cut a window there. He said, "You wash your dishes every day, and all you ever do is look at yourself. You never get beyond your own immediate needs. You need to look through a window so you can see life in a wider perspective." Some of us never get beyond our own needs, and negativism takes over our perspective because we see life only from our selfish needs and not from the wider angle of including other people in the picture.

Disbelief

A major reason that we lose a sense of the vision of God is disbelief. The Israelites saw their faith grow weak as they thought about the giants before them. The disciples were not able to perform a miracle, Jesus said, because their faith was too weak. We know something about our own faith seeming to dissipate on occasion, don't we?

Sometimes our faith appears to disappear in the midst of crises, difficulties, and problems, because they seem overwhelming and we do not know where to turn.

In the small book *Children's Letters to God*, one of the children wrote, "Dear Mr. God. How do you feel about people who don't believe in you? Somebody else wants to know. A friend. Neil." God, how do you feel about people who don't believe in you? Especially people who claim to believe in you? What do you think about people, God, when they get in crises of life where they are experiencing suffering, pain, and difficulties and they find it hard to believe? When the whole world seems to be crashing around us, God, how do you feel about us? God, of course, knows that we human beings are weak. Before we are too hard on the Israelites, let's remember they had been slaves in Egypt and had wandered in the wilderness for forty years while they were searching, groping, and hoping for the promised land. Sometimes our faith, like theirs, is too small.

The Importance of a Small Faith

The supreme lesson in this story is that even the smallest amount of faith is transforming in the lives of individuals. Caleb and Joshua had faith in God that they could be victorious if they went into the new territory (Num 14:24). Remember that Jesus said to his disciples, "If you have faith as a grain of mustard seed, you can remove mountains." Mustard seeds are tiny seeds. They look almost like specks of pepper. Jesus drew his image from the tiniest thing known to the people in that part of the world. "If you have the tiniest speck of faith," Jesus declared, "you have the possibility of removing gigantic obstacles." The mountain was a Jewish metaphor for difficulty. The image was not to be taken literally. If you sit down one day and say, "I'll see if I've got enough faith to remove that mountain across the road from my house," then you have missed the point of this image. For ancient Jewish people, a mountain was symbolic of great difficulties. If you have the smallest amount of faith, you have the assurance that God will help you meet any difficulty.

Faith Has Moved Mountains

Faith has moved mountains in the past. Faith has removed kings. It has transformed empires. Faith has changed pagan culture. Faith has changed individuals. Faith has overcome mountains of greed, prejudice, selfishness, hostility, drunkenness, and laziness. Faith has removed all kinds of mountains in the past, and faith has also built churches, hospitals, universities, children's homes, and other creative agencies down through the centuries to help individuals live a better life. Faith has moved mountains, and faith has also built mountains of goodness in many places.

When we have even a small seed of faith, God begins to cut the giants down to size. If we live with the grasshopper approach to life, everything seems gigantic, but when we have a small amount of faith, it begins to give us a new perspective on the giant difficulties that loom before us. We know we do not face them alone. We face our giants with the assurance of the power, presence, and strength of God to enable us to meet them. "This is the victory that overcomes the world," the Scriptures say, "our faith." Faith brings alive the power of Christ within us to enable us to face giants. Its transforming power, even as a speck, makes a great difference.

The Disciples' Lack of Faith Transformed

Although the disciples could not cure the young boy down in the valley below the mountain, later they were able to perform miracles in the name of Christ. As Peter and the other disciples went forth to minister, they had healing powers through the presence of Christ. They cured people. The same disciples who did not have enough faith to heal before the resurrection went forth after the resurrection with a great faith, and they transformed the world and turned it upside down in the name of Jesus Christ. You know that in your own life there have been instances when you have felt the presence of God. You may have reached out with only a tiny speck of faith, but today you can affirm the difference it made. "Oh Lord," the father said in the valley, "I believe, help thou my unbelief." And we make the same cry! Even a tiny bit of belief is sufficient to transform the mountains that block our paths. Let's believe so Christ can do his work through us.

We have all read stories about individuals who were caught in some traumatic situation. A father, for example, discovers his young son is trapped under a car, and he reaches down and literally lifts the car off the child. The child is pulled out safely, and later the father tries to lift the car and he cannot budge it. How does that happen? Where does he get the strength? We don't know for sure. Experts say that, in a crisis, individuals are sometimes able to get an enormous surge of hidden physical strength that they did not know they had. They draw upon this latent strength to do an impossible feat in a sudden moment. These instances indicate the tremendous resources that we have within our body, mind, and spirit that are almost never tapped. How can we draw them forth from the hidden chambers of our inner lives? Don't we wish we knew how we could do it? But isn't a part of what Christ is telling us here that we begin to draw on this hidden power with a tiny seed of faith? That seed is the secret of bringing forth the powers within us.

An Inner Vision of Faith

But it all depends on our vision. Caleb believed the children of Israel could be victorious with the power of God working through them. Later biblical references like Numbers indicate that Caleb did find victory and claim new land. Look at a modern example. A man wrote to a friend who had been sick and said he was sorry to learn that he had been severely ill for several months, and he hoped that his Christian faith had been able to sustain him during his illness. The friend wrote back and said that he had been miserable during his illness. Everything that could possibly be wrong with him had gone wrong. And no, his religion had not done anything for him, because he had not gone to church since he was a young child. He remained miserable.

But the man who had written him also wrote to another friend and expressed to him the hope that his faith had strengthened him. His other friend wrote back and said, "Yes, I have been in difficult circumstances recently and have been quite ill, but the thing that has enabled me to endure it has been the sense of the presence of God in my life. He has sustained me." What a difference in their inner vision on life!

When I walk with people during the crises of their lives, it is so tragic to witness those who have nothing to lean back on because they have made no preparation in good days to experience the power of God in their lives. They have no real experience of faith to sustain them. The tiny seed of faith could enable them to meet the great giants that will confront them along life's paths. Our faith can make the difference, even if it is small.

The Heavy Demands of Faith

Notice, finally, that the demands that come to us about faith seem unattainable. Caleb knew that victory would not be easy because of the strength of their enemies, but he trusted in the power of God to meet the heavy challenge. "Caleb became the exponent of a fearless faith in the God," R. F. Johnson notes, "who had promised Israel land."[1] The Christian faith presents us with giant challenges. For example, Jesus has told us that we are supposed to love our enemies. Who among us loves our enemies as we should? He instructed us "to do unto others as we would have them do unto us." Who among us does that completely? He commanded us to love our neighbors. Who among us loves our neighbors fully? Christ has challenged us to be his servants in the world. Who among us is totally serving? Jesus has told us to "seek first the kingdom of God and everything else will be added unto us." Who among us truly seeks first the kingdom of God? Jesus has declared that we are to be perfect as our heavenly Father is perfect. Who among us is completely perfect?

These goals seem unattainable, and yet Jesus Christ has lifted them before us to challenge us as we follow him. We may begin with the smallest kind of faith, like Caleb, but then we continue to move toward the highest faith that we can have by God's grace. We are challenged to reach for the highest, the farthest, and the greatest possibilities of what we can be. We may fall short, but we do not settle for the lowest goal we can achieve or a negative goal but for the highest, the best, and the most positive.

Michelangelo had a famous student whose name was Raphael. One day Michelangelo came to see some of Raphael's paintings and noticed a painting on an easel in which all the figures seemed small, faint, and indistinguishable. He took a brush and wrote across the painting, "Amplius!" "Larger!" He wanted the younger artist to know that if he were going to paint pictures, he had to quit trying to paint everything in its smallest perspective but instead to see people, trees, and all of life in their largest possibilities.

Too many of us have a vision that is too narrow, too small, or too negative. We need to learn through the power of Christ to let our vision be expanded to include our brother, our sister, and our enemy. All of us, as we draw on the "seed of faith" within us, have the strength that is sufficient to meet these giants, whatever shape or form they may take. Do not give way to the negative, but allow the small seed of faith to grow into a mighty tree of faith to sustain you in your hour of need.

8

David: The Lamb and Lion of Israel

1 Samuel 17:31-40

The noted Scottish preacher Alexander Maclaren wrote in his book, *The Life of David*, that "David is like his own harp of many chords through which the breath of God murmured, drawing forth wailing and rejoicing, the clear ring of triumphant trust, the low plaint of penitence, the blended harmonies of all devout emotions."[1] David had a many-sided personality and has been the source of various images for the Hebrew people. As a shepherd lad, he symbolized to the nation of Israel the importance of the laboring man. As a warrior, he freed Israel from the Goliaths who threatened its borders. As a victorious general, he at times showed the ruthlessness of his age to his enemies, and at other times he demonstrated a magnanimous spirit. He was a musician whose melodies soothed a deranged king and earned him the title of the "sweet singer of Israel." Many of the psalms pulsate with the haunting lyrics from his poetic hand. As king, he united the nation of Israel and stretched its borders further than any king of Israel ever would.

Sixty-two chapters in the Bible are devoted to a biography of David. There are more than eight hundred references to David in the Old Testament and sixty in the New Testament. Some scholars believed that David's name originally was Elhanan (2 Sam 21:19) and that he assumed the name David when he ascended the throne. One of the interesting facts about the Bible is that it always presents people with warts and all. The Bible notes the greatness of David but does not hesitate to describe his weaknesses as well. It presents David at his greatest moments but also at his weakest.

Another Scottish preacher, George Matheson, a minister of St. Bernard Church in Edinburgh, made the following observation about David:

> I believe this man epitomized not only the past history, but the past passions, of Israel. I believe the two streams of heredity which had run in separate channels for the path of the nation met at last in a single life—the life of David. If I were to christen these two streams, I would call them "The Lion" and "The Lamb." Look back over the history of the Hebrew race, and you will find the mortal life of that race ever depicted as a strife between two. Go where you will, you are ever confronted by a pair. Every lamb has its opposing lion. Abel has his Cain; Abraham has his Lot; Isaac his Ishmael; Jacob has his Esau; Joseph has his "Brethren"; Moses his Amalek; Joshua his Achan. In David the two pass into one. He became the heir to a double heredity. The strings of his life-harp are swept by two impulses—a south wind and a north—the one bringing music, the other discord.[2]

As Matheson indicates, David's life depicts the two streams of life—one positive, one negative—and the constant struggle between the two. This is depicted as "the Lamb" and "the Lion" in the life of David. David's life reflects his ongoing pilgrimage, wrestling with the choices of the good or the bad.

The Anointing of David

I invite you to travel with me through some of the Old Testament pages that give the story of David. The mark that he left on Israel and the Christian church is immense, and many people have walked down the path that he cut centuries ago. The story of David begins in a small village called Bethlehem, a few miles from Jerusalem. One day some of the villagers noticed that the prophet Samuel was coming up the road toward their city. He walked with a staff in one hand, and a goat's horn filled with oil was tied to a cord over his shoulder. He drove a heifer in front of him. As he approached the village, some of the leaders were frightened, since this prophet usually did not come to Bethlehem. "Are you coming on peaceful business?" they asked. "Yes," he assured them. "My visit is peaceful." Quietly he summoned Jesse and told him that God had sent him on a mission, and he would like to meet Jesse's sons. Jesse was the father of ten children, eight sons and two daughters. Samuel did not disclose the nature of the mission.

Samuel probably had the villagers prepare the heifer for sacrifice while he met the sons of Jesse. God had told Samuel that he was displeased with Saul, whose spirit had departed from him, and told Samuel to anoint the son of Jesse whom God would designate. As the eldest son approached, Samuel noticed that he was a tall, handsome, strong young man. He thought to himself that surely this was God's chosen one. It seems amazing to me that Samuel so quickly thought that someone who was tall and handsome, like Saul, would be God's chosen one. But the inner voice of God was silent. All seven sons walked past Samuel. God was still silent. Samuel was disappointed and could not understand. He thought he had come to this village at God's direction to anoint the next king.

Perplexed, he asked Jesse, "Do you have any other sons?" "Yes, there is a young son in the fields taking care of the sheep." "Would you bring him here?" Jesse sent for David, and in a few minutes David came running up the road. Samuel saw a youth, probably sixteen years old or younger, with a slingshot over his shoulder and his shepherd's staff in his hand. As David approached the prophet, Samuel saw a young lad, who was handsome, with ruddy (dark) cheeks, and bright eyes (1 Sam 16:12). When Samuel saw David, the inner voice of God communicated to him that "This is the man." At this moment Samuel was informed that God looks on the inward and not the outward appearance of people. He selects those who may appear to be insignificant by the world's standards. Samuel asked David to kneel and anointed his head with the oil without revealing to him the purpose. His brothers watched with anger and jealousy. That secret anointing was the beginning of David's pilgrimage to be king of Israel.

Music for King Saul

The next scene in which we see David, he is invited to play his harp in the palace before Saul. King Saul has become melancholy and is wrestling with depression. Someone in his court has heard of this "sweet singer of songs" and player of musical instruments, and so David is invited to come to the palace and sing and play for the king. David does so, and Saul makes David one of his personal attendants or armor-bearers.

David Confronts Goliath

This scene quickly changes to the familiar story about David's encounter with Goliath. Scholars have noted that there is some confusion in these two stories. Some feel that there may be two different traditions here about how David first entered Saul's court. In the Goliath story, Saul doesn't seem to know David. Yet David has been playing and singing songs in the palace and was Saul's armor-bearer. Why doesn't Saul know him? It is not clear how much time passed. Maybe David went home for a while and Saul did not recognize him when they met again. Or maybe these two stories are from different traditions and the chronicler did not try to harmonize them.

Jesse called David in from the fields where he was keeping sheep and asked him to take some food to his brothers who were away engaged in military service in a battle with the Philistines. The battle had been at a standstill for forty days as the giant Goliath taunted Israel. The Philistines were on one side of the valley of Elah, and Israel was stationed on the other. Goliath challenged Israel, "Send your bravest man to fight me. Where is your champion?" Goliath stood nine and a half feet tall and was covered from head to foot in plated armor. He probably looked something like a soldier in one of Homer's stories. Frederick Buechner observed that "this giant not only looked like a Sherman tank but weighed like one."[3] He stood there covered with that brass-plated armor, taunting Israel.

Then along came David, filled with the enthusiasm of youth. "I think I can battle this guy!" he announced. His brothers immediately cried, "Shut up! Be quiet! Who do you think you are?" After a while David's desire to fight the giant was reported to Saul. By this time, Saul must have been desperate, and he sent for David. When he saw David, he told him, "How can you fight this man? You are not a trained soldier. He has been a soldier since his youth. What makes you possibly think you can defeat him?" David told Saul about his experiences as a shepherd with lions and bears and how he had defeated them with his sling or barehanded. But the underlying emphasis in David's argument is not his own strength but the fact that God was with him.

I wonder if the thought throbbing in Saul's mind was that God was no longer with him. Once he was filled with confidence about what he could do with the strength of God helping him. Now he heard another youth declaring with assurance that God was with him. Maybe Saul remembered when he felt that way. I am not certain why Saul chose to let David go battle Goliath, but he did.

Saul attempted to equip David for battle in his own armor. It is unclear why David could not wear the king's armor. Was it because he was young, and it was too big for him? Maybe or maybe not. Even as a youth, David may have been a large young man. It could be that he just wasn't used to it. We don't know the reason for certain. But the king's armor was too cumbersome for him. Like Saul, those of us who are older adults often try to put our armor, our equipment, our clothes, and our perspective on the younger generation. We expect them to do things the way we do them and according to our interpretations. But it usually doesn't work.

David put Saul's armor aside and went out to the valley to meet the giant Goliath. When the giant saw this young lad running toward him, he cried, "What am I, a dog, that you would send this small kid to battle me? I will kill him and feed him to the birds!" Goliath moved toward David slowly under the weight of his armor. He approached him with a spear, javelin sword, and shield. His body was covered in all places except his "Achilles' heel," his forehead. David reached down in the stream and picked up five smooth stones. He put one of the stones in his sling and ran toward the giant. David cried out, "You come to me with a sword, a spear, and a shield. But I come to you in the name of the LORD of hosts, the God of the armies of Israel.

This day God will deliver you into my hand." As he raced toward the giant, his dark hair trailed behind him like a sunbeam. Suddenly he sent a stone flying like the speed of light from his slingshot. It landed in the forehead of the giant. Goliath fell with a thud to the ground. Did he see in his final brief moments this fleet-as-a-deer youth rushing up to him without a weapon in his hands? Then David picked up Goliath's own sword and cut off the giant's head.

David's Conflict with King Saul

After his triumphant victory, David was lauded as a great hero. He had said that this victory was for the glory of God, but David certainly got a lot of praise and admiration from it. Soon, as David sang his sweet songs to Saul, the king grew overcome with envy and threw his javelin at David and tried to kill him. The common people were singing their own songs: "Saul has slain his thousands but David his tens of thousands." Soon the fame of David increased to the point of causing a real conflict with the king. He became insanely jealous of David. Saul tried to get his son Jonathan and his servants to kill David. But Jonathan and David had become good friends. These two had such a bonded friendship that Jonathan even warned David when his father Saul plotted to kill him. On one occasion Jonathan worked out a warning based on how far he shot some arrows in the air. "If I shoot the arrows far into the field and tell my servant they are beyond him, that means that my father is still angry and wants to kill you. A short distance will mean all is forgiven." He shot the arrows a great distance, warning David. The two of them remained friends until the death of Jonathan.

On other occasions, Saul sent some of his soldiers to capture David at Ramah and even tried to seize him there himself. On hearing that Saul was plotting to kill David, David's wife Michal, the daughter of Saul, let him down over the wall by a rope through a window, and David escaped.

From that point for over a year, David was a fugitive—an outlaw. The king and his soldiers continuously hunted for him. He escaped first to Nob, where the high priest befriended him. It is thought that Nob was established by the priests who fled when Shiloh was destroyed. At the time of David, about eighty-five priests lived there (1 Sam 22:18). David arrived at Nob with nothing. He pleaded with Ahimelech, the high priest, for food. "All I have here is holy bread," Ahimeleck replied, "and your men can have it if they have kept themselves pure." David indicated that he and his men had maintained the ritual of sexual purity during this time, but he did not even have any men with him. He then took the bread of the Presence. Later Jesus defended his own action on the Sabbath by referring to this story.

Then David indicated that he did not even have a weapon. The priest stated that the only weapon he had was the sword of Goliath, which was wrapped in a cloth behind the ephod. The young man, David, arrived without any weapons or possessions. He took the sword of Goliath that he had used to cut off the giant's head. When he fled from Saul, David was alone and without weapons, but soon he would return with a whole army of men behind him. After several skirmishes with Saul's soldiers, David fled as a refugee into Philistine territory to the city of Ziklag. He made Ziklag his base and operated out of it for almost a year. The Philistines thought that David had become one of their vassals. What the Philistines did not know was that, instead of killing Israelites, David was attacking the Philistines and displaying bounty captured in raids on them. When David attacked the Philistines, he brought back no prisoners, so the Philistines did not realize that he had been attacking them. During his year in Ziklag, he slowly formed a small army of men around him.

One time when Saul was searching for David, he camped at Engedi. David was nearby in a cave and slipped up to where Saul was sleeping with his soldiers. David could have killed the king right then, but he refused. Instead, he cut off a part of the king's robe to indicate how close he had been to him. The next morning David approached Saul and revealed the part he had cut off from his robe. "I could have killed you," David said, "but I did not, because you are God's anointed." David did not want to seize the throne by assassination. Although Saul indicated in that moment a feeling of devotion to David, it did not last, and he continued his open conflict with David.

When David and his band of men went to fight with the Philistines against Israel, some of the Philistines cried, "We can't trust David to be on our side. Send him away." This action kept David from having to show his true colors at that time. So David and his soldiers returned home. When they got back, they found their villages a smoldering ruin. The Amalekites had raided their base and destroyed it, carrying off all their possessions, wives, and children. Others had been killed. And everything of value had been taken. After this painful event, David's men were ready to stone him. The Scriptures tell us that David "strengthened himself in the LORD" (1 Sam 30:6). He found the inner strength of God's presence when he had lost everything. Everything! He had lost his family, his house, and his possessions. But he had not lost his God. He rallied his soldiers around him, and guided them in pursuit of the enemy. They overtook the Amalekites, surprised them, killed them, rescued their own families, and retrieved all their possessions.

A few days later, in the heat of battle when he saw that all was lost, Saul fell on his own sword and committed suicide. Jonathan was also killed in that same battle on the plain of Esdraelon. When David learned of the death of Saul and Jonathan, he was filled with grief and composed a moving tribute. The entire poem is found in 2 Samuel 1:19-27. "Saul and Jonathan, beloved and lovely! In life and in death they were not divided; they were swifter than eagles, they were stronger than lions," David wrote (2 Sam 19:23).

David Crowned as King

At this point the nation of Israel was without a king. David prayed and went to Hebron where he was crowned king of Judah. For seven and a half years he ruled as king of Judah from Hebron. Following Saul's death, Saul's only surviving son Ishbosheth was made king, under the strong leadership of his powerful military leader Abner, over all the tribes of Israel except Judah. Ishbosheth reigned for a short period of time before he was murdered by two of his own officers. They rushed to inform David of their assassination, hoping to be rewarded, but David condemned their action and had them put to death. After Ishbosheth's death, David was asked to be king of both Judah and Israel, bringing the nation together. Shortly after he became king, Joab captured the city sitting on four hills—Jerusalem—which was 4,000 feet above sea level. Jerusalem was made the capital city of Israel, and David changed its name to Zion, the City of David. Jerusalem, of course, has continued to be the great holy city of Israel. David expanded his kingdom from the Euphrates to Egypt, a territory of 55,000 square miles. This was the largest expansion that the kingdom of Israel ever realized. David reigned for thirty-three years, and for most of this time the nation experienced relative peace.

The Ark of the Covenant

Another important action of David was to bring the ark of the covenant into Jerusalem. This action established Jerusalem as the center of the nation's worship. The ark of the covenant was the closest thing Israel had to some symbolism of their God. David almost turned the bringing of the ark into a circus parade. As the ark was brought into the city, crowds went before it tooting horns, playing other musical instruments, and dancing. When the ark was brought into the city of Zion, David danced before the ark of the covenant with great joy. But his wife Michal, Saul's daughter, a more properly bred woman, did not think that was appropriate behavior for a king, and she chastised him for this action. David, however, was filled with so much enthusiasm that he could not control himself.

David also began making preparations for the building of the temple. Years before, when David fled to Nob to escape Saul's attempt to kill him, the priests gave David some assistance. King Saul killed all of the priests in Nob, except one who escaped. This dastardly action caused the priests to support David. David made Jerusalem not only the political center of power but also the center of religious power as well. Throughout his life, David sought to determine what God wanted him to do. In his heart he was a deeply religious man. When we condemn some of David's actions, we must remember that David probably lived a thousand years before Christ. This means that his reign took place about three thousand years ago. That is a long time. So, when we want to be critical of David and some of his behavior, let's remember that he lived in a primitive world.

David's Sin of Adultery

The darkest chapter in David's life came one night when he walked out on the veranda at his palace. His men were away in battle. He was alone and idle. By nature, he was a restless, emotional man. He looked down from his veranda and saw Bathsheba bathing. Lust overpowered David, and he resolved to have this woman. And what David wanted, David got. Bathsheba responded to the king's command and committed adultery with him. When Bathsheba realized later that she was pregnant, David tried to find some way to avoid disgracing her. David had Uriah, Bathsheba's husband, sent home from the front lines. He thought that if Uriah came home and spent the night with his wife, he would assume that he was the father of the child. But Uriah was too much of a soldier to do that. When he came home, he chose not to spend the night with his wife. He knew that a good soldier did not engage in sexual activity during a military campaign. That trick didn't work. What did David do then? He asked Joab, the commander of his army, to put Uriah at the front of battle where he would surely be killed. Shortly, Uriah was killed. After a reasonable period of time, David took Bathsheba as one of his wives. She remained his favorite.

Some time later, a sense of recognition of David's sin was driven home by Nathan the prophet. Nathan had worked closely with David in many ways before. Nathan told David that he wanted to share a story with him. He told a story about a wealthy man with large herds and flocks. There was another man with only one wee lamb. This lamb was precious to him. He fed this lamb from his own table and held it in his arms at night like a baby. The rich man, who had so many possessions and so many animals of his own, took this man's one lamb and killed it for his dinner.

On hearing this story, David asked, "Who is this man? He should be killed. He should pay back four-fold what he has done." As he reached for his sword, he asked, "Who is this man?" Nathan pointed to him and said, "You are the man." Through this parable, Nathan held up a mirror so David could see his own sin. Many of us are often blind to our own weaknesses and sins. We either can't see them or refuse to see them. Sometimes it takes someone else to open our eyes to them.

David's Repentance

David immediately recognized his sinfulness and repented. His mournful cry is voiced in the Fifty-first Psalm. "I have sinned against God," David cries. "I have not just sinned against this woman. My sin is against God." Nathan had to wonder whether the king would kill him for this bold act. But his courageous act led to David's repentance.

The prophet informed David, "Your repentance is accepted, but there will be results from this action." Consequences for sins cannot be avoided. Even if you and I repent of our sins, we cannot stop the results or consequences that may come from our sins. We may be able to pull nails out of a tree after we have driven them in, but we cannot remove the nail holes from a tree after we remove the nails. Nathan told David that terrible consequences would come to pass because of his sin. "A sword will hang upon your house. . . . This baby will die." The last years of David's life were filled with sorrow and troubles. The baby who came from this act of sin did die. David's son Absalom killed his brother Amnon because he had raped his half-sister, Tamar. Later Absalom led a rebellion to overthrow his father's reign and tried to take the kingdom by force. David had to flee from Jerusalem. David asked Joab to send his army to stop Absalom but begged him not to hurt his son. However, when Joab's army had Absalom's forces in flight, Absalom was caught in a tree while riding under it, and Joab saw his predicament and killed him. He sent a message back to King David that his son was dead.

A great outpouring of grief arose from David. He cried, "Oh, my son, oh, my son Absalom." Forgetting the throne, forgetting his son's lust for power, forgetting that his son was a traitor, forgetting the murder of his other son, forgetting the victory, forgetting his own soldiers and their faithfulness to him, forgetting everything but the loss of a son, he sobbed from the pain of the reality of his death.

David lived to be about seventy years old. On his deathbed he passed his kingdom on to Solomon. Solomon, the son of Bathsheba, a favorite wife, became the next ruler over Israel. This is important for the New Testament. David was concerned that God would take away the messianic role from him as was done to Saul, but God promised otherwise. Nonetheless, the Davidic kingdom line ended with the Babylonian exile. How to reconcile the promise of God and the actuality of the termination of the promise to David led to the postexile hope that when the ultimate Messiah appeared, he would be of the lineage of David. Thus, the genealogies of Matthew and Luke, which disagree on practically every point, are at least in agreement that Jesus must come through the lineage of David. Thus, the promise of YHWH was carried forward.[4]

A Man after God's Own Heart

When Samuel received instruction from God about the one he was to anoint as the new king of Israel, God told him that this new king would be "a man after my own heart." I think the key word here is "after." David certainly did not fully have the heart of God. But he did honestly strive after God and to know God's will for his life. Like all of us, he was human and slipped at times. But his inner resolve to follow God remained with him all his life. Down through the ages, Israel and the Christian church have lauded David as a great poet, warrior, king, and musician, a deeply religious man, and one who has continues to speak to our world today through his joys and sorrows. Later the prophets looked back to David for the long-awaited Messiah. Jesus, our Lord, was called the Son of David. Jesus, like David, was born in Bethlehem. It is interesting that a story about a lamb provoked David's confession of sin. And the gospel story about the "Lamb of God," Jesus Christ, calls men and women today to confess their sins and find the forgiveness of God.

David, the great poet and singer, most likely penned these favorite words of assurance:

> The LORD is my shepherd, I shall not want;
> he makes me lie down in green pastures.

He leads me beside the still waters;
he restores my soul.
He leads me in paths of righteousness for his name's sake.
Even though I walk through the valley of the shadow of death,
I will fear no evil; for thou art with me;
thy rod and thy staff, they comfort me.
Thou preparest a table before me
in the presence of my enemies;
thou anointest my head with oil,
my cup overflows.
Surely goodness and mercy shall follow me
all the days of my life;
and I shall dwell in the house of the LORD forever.
(Psalm 23, King James Version)

Let that be your prayer and mine.

9

Jeremiah: When Life Crashes In

With his head buried in his hands, tears began to flow as Jeremiah vented his innermost feelings. "Oh God, oh God, where are you? Why do you seem so distant from me? Oh, if I had never been born." In his private, personal journal, which was not written for other eyes to see, Jeremiah had recorded his innermost feelings of distress and turmoil. "Oh God," he wrote. "I sat alone, isolated, without anyone caring or knowing where I am." In his journal his feelings seem to leap out. He records feelings of aloneness and anger, frustration and failure, dejection and despondency, despair and doubt, hatred and hostility, ridicule and rejection.

"Oh God," he writes, "where are you in the midst of all my turmoil? I have done what you asked me to do. I responded to your call. I have preached your message, and yet instead of the people receiving it, I have received only rejection and ridicule. God, where are you?" Isolated and alone, Jeremiah struggled with his personal feelings. God's heaven seemed to be made of brass. "I pray to you," he said, "but there seems to be no response. Where are you, God? My words seem to echo off the walls of Jerusalem, rebounding and ringing around in my head. The words I pray to you come back like the hot breath of the desert wind that throws stinging sand against my face. There is no response. Oh God, why do you not answer me? Are you too busy? Are you too kind and understanding, or do you not care? Oh God, why do you not answer me? Why do you leave me in my aloneness?"

A Prophet's Message

Jeremiah had responded to God at an early age. Some scholars have projected that it might have been at the age of fourteen. He answered God's call to preach his message to the nation of Judah. For forty years he proclaimed the destruction of Israel. "Judgment will come from the north, and Jerusalem will fall," he preached. But year after year went by and nothing happened. No enemy came, and no destruction fell upon the people. Jeremiah wanted to get married and have a family, but God said that the end was coming soon and told him not to get married. He was instructed not to engage in social functions. The end did not come quickly, though. Jeremiah waited and waited. While he waited for God's judgment to fall, he was rejected by his friends, the political leaders, and the religious leaders. Even his own family plotted to put him to death. They couldn't understand his strange behavior. They feared being accused of treason because of his prophecy.

The Aloneness of Jeremiah

Jeremiah recorded his personal confessions, and out of his agony he cried, "I sat alone." This is the aloneness of a leper who is isolated from all the rest of society. In his aloneness, Jeremiah longed to sense the presence of God. Too often we think that the ancient prophets always walked in unparalleled fellowship with God. We assume that they felt the strength of God's strong arm by their side at every moment. But Jeremiah in his honesty tells us that this was not always true for him. There were times when he was caught in the floods and storms of life that swept him away from his foundation. He reached for the bottom but could not find it. He groped and searched for a word from God. He reached the point where he questioned his calling, his purpose, his message, and even his God. "Where are you, God?" he cried. "I sat alone."

We, Too, Know Rejection

Jeremiah is not the only one with that kind of experience. You and I have known those kinds of feelings, too. If we are honest, we have to admit that there have been times in our lives when we felt alone and wondered where God was in our pain, rejection, ridicule, loneliness, despair, and depression—moments when, like Jeremiah, we have cried out to God and said, "I sit alone."

There are times in life when we ask, as Jeremiah did, "Are you in heaven, Father? If so, why don't you do something? Why do you not respond to my need, my prayer, my despair?" Jeremiah had experienced rejection. The people had rejected his message and him, and he sat alone in his despair.

Like Jeremiah, we have all known rejection at some time or another. Do you recall the first time you tried to get a date with the person you saw at school? You placed your call to them with great hope, but back came their response: "I'm sorry, not interested." Or you may have sat on the other end of the line waiting for someone to call, and the call never came. Or you may have been the young person who raced to the end zone; you were wide open, and the football hit you right in your arms. You had the winning touchdown in your hands, but you dropped it. Later you had to go back to the locker room and feel the coolness of your teammates. Or you have felt the "cold shoulder" of your coworkers. Or you have watched others walk away without speaking as you approach.

Some have known the rejection of losing a job. You have a sinking feeling. After years of hard work, you are no longer wanted or needed. An awful sense of rejection comes over your life like a dark cloud. Some of you know the feeling of rejection that comes when sides are chosen on the sandlot or in the classroom, and you are the one who is always chosen last. Rejection comes in many shapes and forms, and like Jeremiah, we are too familiar with it. Some of you have experienced it when your marriage failed. You have sensed it when people did not like your ideas or thoughts. Or at work, you have noticed that people discuss you behind your back. Rejection has come into your life, and like Jeremiah, you feel like you have sat alone.

The Sense of Ridicule

People laughed at Jeremiah and mockingly said, "You have preached that destruction was coming upon us soon. It has been thirty-eight years since you began preaching that line, Jeremiah, but nothing has happened yet. You are a fool!" Jeremiah became an object of ridicule.

Like him, many of you have also known ridicule. People have made fun of something you said or did, or the way you look, talk, or walk. I will never forget an experience I had in elementary school. I had been asked to read out loud. While reading, I came across a word I didn't recognize. I probably should have known it, but I didn't. It was a small word—"awe." I mispronounced it. To this day, I can still feel the ridicule I experienced from my teacher as well as the class.

We have all been ridiculed in some way or another. Sometimes children can be devastating in the stinging words they say to each other.

Loneliness

Jeremiah also knew loneliness. He felt isolated from other people and especially from God. Jeremiah had no support group. His family and friends had rejected him. Only one loyal person, his scribe Baruch, stood by him.

But you have known loneliness, too, haven't you? You have known the loneliness of going off to a new city or a new school. You have had to make new friends and adapt to a whole new way of life. It has not been easy. Some of you have known the loneliness of putting your husband or wife or parents in a nursing home. Some of you know the loneliness of eating Thanksgiving or Christmas dinner alone. Some of you know the loneliness of looking across a table each night and seeing an empty chair where a loved one used to sit.

I read about a woman living alone who would wait at night to hear the announcer say his closing words before she turned the radio off and went to sleep. She waited to hear him say, "And I wish to you all a very good night." John Milton said that God proclaimed loneliness as the first thing that was not good: "It is not good for man to be alone." Who among us has not felt loneliness at some point in our lives?

Failure

Jeremiah thought he was a failure. He had preached God's message for thirty-eight years, and he had received only rejection and ridicule from his listeners. He thought he had failed God. But finally, God's message was vindicated. We have all known some kind of failure at times. Who has not experienced failure at school, work, or in some relationships with people?

Suffering

Like Jeremiah, we have also known suffering. Sometimes we have felt pain that comes from hurt and isolation. Some of you have suffered with loved ones for a long time as they have slowly died with cancer. Others have watched their children suffer and die from cancer, leukemia, or other dread diseases. Many of you today bear heavy burdens of one kind or another. You know suffering and its harsh reality. You know too well its pain and hurt. Like Jeremiah, you have poured out rivers of tears. You have groped and searched for an answer. "Is there any hope?" you ask.

Jeremiah's Challenge

What did God say to Jeremiah? Instead of offering him comfort, God gave him a challenge. God said, "Jeremiah, you have been preaching to the people to repent! Turn, and come back to me. Now, what I want you to do is listen to your own preaching. Repent. You turn back to me, and if you turn back, in turning back to me, you will find strength and support." God did not give him an easy answer. It was not a new answer. There was no new word, but it was the old message that asked Jeremiah to examine his own preaching. "Listen to what you have been preaching." God said. "Turn back to me. You repent, and you will find that I am here to sustain you."

It is easy to worship God on a bright, beautiful day. If you can't worship God on a beautiful day, you never will. But can you bow your knee to God in the freezing cold, zero-degree weather? Can you bow your knee to God when the temperature is at 110 degrees? When your house is on fire, can you worship God? When your ship is sinking, can you worship God? Is God still a strong force when life is hard and the waves of difficulties beat upon the ship of your life? When the storms rage and crash around you, is the presence of God still strong in your life?

That great hurricane of a preacher, Arthur John Gossip, a Scottish minister, experienced the sudden and unexpected death of his wife. After many weeks of struggling with his grief, he was finally able to return to his duties. The first time he entered the pulpit, he spoke about the death of his wife. He said, "Some people asked me, 'Why didn't you fling away from God?'" "In heaven's name," he said, "fling away to what? . . . You people in the sunshine may believe the faith, but we in the shadows must believe it. We have nothing else."[1]

Fling away to what? When you come to the shadows of life—when you come to dark moments and difficult days—that's when you need to reach out and feel the presence of God. Turn. Turn back to God and discover that God is there closer than the breath within you. Feel God's presence. God wants to sustain you.

Distinguish Between the Real and the Artificial

God spoke again to Jeremiah: "Distinguish between the artificial and the real. Separate the superficial and artificial from the genuine and vital." What a needed word for us today. Too many of us have been hooked by sentimental and artificial religion. When our religion is only artificial and we experience the storms of life, we find ourselves sinking. Many people think that God is someone they can manipulate and control. These people have bought into the lie that the religious life is basically the "get-rich-quicker" life. If you are religious and say the "right words," God will make you rich and happy. Or if you just think positive thoughts, everything will be all right. When difficulties come into your life, though, this superficial religion crumbles and is not able to sustain you.

I knew a woman who always had easy answers for everybody else's difficult problems. If somebody became ill, she had a quick, pat answer for it. If somebody had trouble, no matter what it was, she thought she could solve it by quoting some verse of Scripture. But one day her husband came down with cancer and slowly died. She had to reach back at that point and see if her sentimental, artificial religion could sustain her. She discovered that only a genuine faith could undergird her. When she sat alone, her faith was tested to see if it was strong and real or only artificial talk.

God's Spokesperson

God spoke further to Jeremiah: "If you will turn to me and separate the genuine from the artificial, you will become my voice. You will be my spokesperson. You will be *my mouth* to proclaim my word to the people." Was Jeremiah tempted to tell the people what they wanted to hear? After preaching God's message and being faithful so long, was he later tempted simply to give the people whatever they wanted and not be true to what he understood the message of God to be? God told him, "If you will turn to me, you will receive strength and support." Only if Jeremiah preached God's genuine message would he continue to be God's voice. The real word of God always takes on fleshy form.

Most of us first "saw" God through other people. We saw through their lives a genuine faith that turned us toward God. We all get tired of seeing people whose religion is artificial and a sham. They have religion only on bright days. We look instead for "living epistles" whose Christianity has invaded their whole lives.

I know a couple who was faithful and active in church. He had served as a deacon. They both had taught Sunday school, served on committees, and worked with young people for years. They were considered by many an ideal Christian young couple. Their eighteen-year-old son went off to college. The first week he was at college he was killed in a tragic accident. Everybody undergirded them with support. Many wondered how they would face this tragedy. But they faced it bravely and courageously, with the strength of God undergirding them. Years later, I asked this couple to talk with others who had to walk through a dark valley. They had a genuine faith that sustained them in their times of difficulty. Now others would listen to them, and they could help them. Their faith in "the dark night" of their soul had enabled them to be a "voice"—a genuine spokesperson for God.

The Support of God

God told Jeremiah, "If you will do these things you will be like a bronzed wall. You will find that your words will be vindicated. I will fortify and sustain you." For Jeremiah, God would not be like a Palestinian wadi, a brook that had water only in springtime. God would be a living, raging stream that always gave him support and encouragement. Centuries later, Jesus told his disciples, "I am alone, yet I am not alone." He had the certainty of his Father's presence.

Jeremiah found that in his aloneness he was not alone. And neither are you or I. There is nothing—absolutely nothing—that can separate us from the presence of God. God is ever present to sustain us. All we have to do is turn and recognize that God is present to undergird and support us. When life crashes in, turn to God like Jeremiah did, and you will discover that God is already seeking to nourish you, nurture you, love you, and sustain you. You do not have to bear your burdens alone. God is there to support you.

10

Balaam: Lessons from the Narrow Places of Life

Numbers 22:21-35

The story found in the book of Numbers about Balaam and his donkey is one of those difficult passages in the Old Testament. For some folks, it is clear evidence that the Scriptures are an ancient relic with absolutely no meaning for us today. For others, it is a clear sign of the miraculous within the Scriptures. How do we deal with a passage that has a talking animal?

The Setting of the Story

Let us capture first something of the setting of that story. The children of Israel were moving like a conquering army through what we call the Holy Land today. To acquire that land, they had to conquer each small tribe as they moved through it. As they drew near the tribe of Moab, King Balak became frightened as he saw the approaching army. So he summoned to his side Balaam, who was a seer, a visionary, a prophet, or a soothsayer. He was not an Israelite. God would work through him and other non-Jews like Cyrus and Ruth. His hand could not be limited to one nation.

When Balaam first received the message from the king of Moab and realized that he wanted him to place a curse on Israel and bring harm to them, he refused. Balak felt that Balaam simply needed some more inducement, so he offered him bigger and better possessions if he would come and curse the Israelites. Balaam said he would pray about the matter again, but even if "Balak were to give me his house full of silver and gold, I could not go beyond the command of the LORD my God, to do less or more." He had decided at first that he would not go, because he had received a message in a dream or vision that God was not going to curse Israel but bless them. Then God directed him the second time to go anyway and talk to the king of Moab.

Balaam began his journey and traveled through a narrow pass toward the city of Moab. The animal on which he was traveling saw an angel with a flaming sword standing in the pathway, and she attempted to turn aside. In the drama of this biblical presentation, three times a similar thing happened until finally the animal found herself in a narrow place with no place to turn around or go off the road. The animal then fell down and rolled over on Balaam. Balaam got up and addressed the animal angrily, and at this point the animal spoke. If the ancient Israelites were hearing or reading this story, they would have found it hilarious. It is presented in a form called narrative folklore. Balaam did not seem surprised, nor did he express any wonder at the animal's ability to speak. This indicates the nature of this ancient drama. The important fact to the listener was the message and not the medium of the message. The important thing is not that the animal spoke but what she had to say!

In several other places in the Scriptures, one reads about trees speaking and snakes talking. Here a donkey talks. Disney has had many animals talk in numerous cartoons. Snoopy, Garfield, and Calvin's stuffed tiger Hobbes all speak. Remember Ed, the talking horse in the TV program of a few decades ago? To the Israelites, this story would have been filled with humor, a type of cartoon for its day. Balaam, who was pompous and overly confident, was not an Israelite, yet he was depicted as being used by the God of Israel. His own animal, a donkey, had to tell this pompous "religious seer" about the presence of God because he was unable to see him. Our problem is that often we cannot hear the story because of the literalism of it, and we become trapped by it and seek to make it historical instead of hearing the ancient message, delivered through the medium of humorous folklore to ancient people with a truth about the presence of God that many often miss.

After the animal spoke, Balaam did see the angel, and the angel told him that he was going against what God wanted him to do. That statement seems troublesome to us, because hadn't God told him to go to Moab with a message? We do not know exactly what had happened, but in some way the message was distorted by Balaam, and he was attempting to do something God did not want him to do. His pompous attitude had left him blind to the warnings of God along the way.

A New Testament Story

There is a story in the New Testament about Jesus talking with two of his disciples on the road to Emmaus after the resurrection (Luke 24:13-35). The disciples could not believe the reports they had heard and were baffled, confused, and depressed. Jesus walked along with them on the short journey from Jerusalem to Emmaus, which was about seven miles, and while traveling there he unfolded the Scriptures to them. They did not know who he was until later he broke bread with them, and then their eyes were opened so they could recognize him.

These two stories have some messages I think we ought to hear today and carry with us. Let me suggest the following lessons.

A False Sense of Independence

The first lesson is that Balaam represents one who felt like he could live his life in total independence. He felt that his own self-reliance and direction were sufficient. We are not sure what message he received from God, but in some way or another he twisted and distorted it, and he decided to carry his own word as the word from God. He felt like he could rely on his own strength, his own understanding, his own methods, and his own ways. He was sufficient. He felt that he did not need to rely just on God's word. God confronted him with his message and directed that he was to share that and not his own words. Many of us today are like Balaam. We go through life thinking that our own self-reliance, our own self-sufficiency, and our own independence can take us through every situation. We believe that we do not need the power and presence of God, nor do we need other people. But none of us is self-made or totally self-sufficient.

When Napoleon was planning the Battle of Waterloo, he instructed his soldiers about where he wanted his artillery, cavalry, and infantry placed. One of his aides asked him, "Should we not consider what the divine might want in this? After all, man proposes and God disposes." Napoleon lifted up his short self, and in his own arrogant way he responded, "Sir, Napoleon proposes, Napoleon disposes." But that very battle proved his undoing. The one who thought that he could always make his own decisions and set his own will against nations soon found that he was defeated.

Too often we attempt to set our own will, purpose, and way against God. To these people, it doesn't make any difference what God might want or what guidance other individuals might want to give us; they alone make the decision. When we try to live life this way, we often find that it collapses around us because we are not open to the power and presence of God's direction. We have made ourselves the only source of guidance, and that may be a path that becomes blocked by our blind selfishness. Many of us live as though there were no God.

A Scottish shepherd once said that when sheep are caught in a blizzard, they can live seven or eight days off their own wool. But if the blizzard continues too long, they will freeze to death. When we attempt to live off our own resources, not drawing on the power and presence of God and not using the resources of other people to guide us, we soon find that we lose our stability, and we may encounter the presence of God who blocks our way.

Encountering God in Unexpected Places

Notice also in these stories that these people met God in unexpected places. Balaam thought he already had a message from God. After all, he had a vision, and now he was traveling to deliver that message to the king of Moab. But he met God unexpectedly in a narrow place of life. The disciples thought that everything was over in their dream about the coming Messiah. They felt defeated and depressed, and while they were on the road to Emmaus going home, Christ walked with them and later revealed himself to them.

Often God encounters us in unexpected places. We had not anticipated him; we had not planned it, yet God "appears" and he is present, and he touches our lives. Moses was attending sheep on a mountainside when suddenly a bush began to burn and the presence of God confronted him. Jacob was fleeing from his brother to save his life when he encountered God in a wilderness place. Isaiah went to the temple grieving because of the loss of his beloved king, and in that experience of worship he met God. Jeremiah was on a casual walk when he saw an almond tree blooming, and from that ordinary experience he had a vision of God. While Paul was traveling on the road to Damascus to persecute and put to death the early Christians, he met the very Christ whom he was seeking to defeat, and his life was changed by him. Down through history, people have encountered God in all kinds of places.

Sometimes you and I meet God in strange places. We may meet him in our affliction and illness, in our work, on the playground, in the gym, or in a school classroom or at a ballgame, in our living room, on the patio, in a conversation with a friend or a stranger, on a trip, or in church. We meet God in all kinds of places. Sometimes unexpectedly, he comes into our lives. We may be washing the dishes, changing a tire, doing our daily work, helping a friend, ill with disease, recovering from surgery, or whatever, when suddenly the very presence of God comes into our lives. we had not anticipated it nor expected it, but it comes.

I recall standing by the bedside of a young fourteen-year-old girl who was dying. Her family had gathered around her. I thought there was going to be only depression and despair. Suddenly, in that moment of tragedy, the whole family, including myself, was gripped with a strong affirmation of the presence of God. I have been beside the beds of people when they were in their last hours, and I have sensed great peace and strength from them because they had an awareness of the presence of God. Sometimes in the narrow places of life we encounter the unexpected presence of God as he comes to meet us and assist us.

Places I Met God

I can recall some beautiful places where I have also met God. I met God in the fellowship hall of my home church, where I made my profession of faith as a fifteen-year-old boy. There God's spirit moved into my life. Later while working in scout camps in the Blue Ridge Mountains of Virginia, I would get up early and walk through the mountain trails to a small lake and sense the awesome presence of Another. While I worked one summer in the Hawaiian Islands, the beauty and splendor there spoke to me of the presence of God. Looking down on my newborn children and grandchildren and seeing the life that I had a small part in creating, I experienced something about the presence and power of God. In unexpected, narrow places, and sometimes in beautiful places, we may find God.

A minister said once that in the community where he lived there was a store called the "Surprise Shop." The shop advertised items for those eight to eighty, and it encouraged people to come and browse. They continued to attract visitors because people were surprised at what was there.[1] Life is often a "Surprise Shop." I think God meets us again and again in surprising places. In unexpected places and in unexpected ways, he speaks to us. It may be in a narrow pass, or it may be on a beautiful, lovely day.

A Word of Judgment

But notice also in these stories that the word of God came in judgment. Balaam met the angel of God. Here, the word "angel" is translated from the Hebrew word for "adversary." God confronted Balaam as his adversary because God came in judgment. Balaam was going to Balak with the wrong message. We are not certain how the message became distorted. It is uncertain whether Balaam was going there to misrepresent what God had told him to say. Was he going there to curse the people of Israel and not to bless them? Had he assumed that his message was God's message? That has become the curse of too many preachers. We turn our opinion into God's word. Too many believe that whatever they think and whatever their opinion is automatically is God's opinion.

Is that what had happened to Balaam? We do not know for certain, but he is confronted by the angel of God. God told him to go and deliver only what he had told him to say. God confronted him in judgment. And in the New Testament story, as the disciples are walking on the road to Emmaus in disbelief, perplexity, and despair, they are met by the Christ who judges their lack of faith by opening the Scriptures to them and telling them about the power of what God has done.

Before you and I can sense the power of God, he first comes in judgment into our lives. He comes in judgment to change us and direct us to open our lives so our sinfulness can be transformed by his power. He calls us to be more like what he has created us to be.

I read about a preacher who served in a small rural church. He was known for his large size, strength, and athletic ability. One day two teenagers came into his church and were disruptive while he was trying to preach. He finally stopped his sermon and said to these two young men, "If you guys didn't come here to listen, why did you come?" They said, "We came to see a miracle." The big preacher walked down from the pulpit, reached over and got them both by the collar, pitched them out the door, and said, "We don't perform miracles here; we cast out devils."

Sometimes in our churches, before miracles are performed there must be the casting out of demons and devils. The sinfulness within us has to move out before God's spirit can sweep through our lives and make us clean and whole. One of the tragedies today is that too often we think we can keep on sinning without turning to God, repenting, or changing and still be a loyal church member. Too many continue to do things that are displeasing to God without making any effort to change. God comes into our lives to bring love and grace and redemption. But if our lives are constantly filled with hatred and sin of all kinds, he cannot communicate his love and grace. First he must cast out the evil spirits within us so that his grace can fill us with love, hope, and righteousness. When our lives are filled with lies, distrust, and hatred, God cannot fill us with grace, hope, love, and mercy. He first comes in judgment. The holiness of God cannot stand in the presence of sin. He must purge it, transform it, and cleanse it.

A church youth worker was walking on a beach one day and saw one of his teenagers wearing a T-shirt. When the young man saw his leader, he immediately crossed his arms. The leader walked up to him and said, "Oh, you have on one of those T-shirts with a message. I can't quite read what it says. Does it say, 'University of Virginia'?" The young man looked down and said, "No." "Well, let me see," the man said. The youth dropped his arms, and written on the shirt were these words: "Stamp out virginity." The church youth worker looked at him sadly and started to walk away. The teenager dropped in step beside him and said, "If you don't think I ought to wear it, I'll take it off." The worker said, "I have a better suggestion. Why don't you take it home and have it laundered and put in a bag? You look like a young man that one of these days is going to get married and have a family. Save it, and when your daughter goes on her first date, I want you to give it to her then." The young man looked back at the youth worker and said, "I get your message. If my father had said that to me, I would never have worn it."

When does the church stand up and pronounce judgment against the sinfulness of much of our modern day's distortion of sex? It is not okay to do anything we want, anyplace, anywhere, anytime. The sense of sanctity about sex needs to be recovered. The Christian lifestyle is often not what is depicted on much of our television sets and movies as free sex and free love. Free sex is never free. It is always costly. Many times young people are never told what its price tag is. As in this situation with the teenager, the word from God may come to us as judgment. God comes as the change agent to transform us by his spirit. So God may first come as an adversary to tell us our lives need to be different. As we walk with the God who is the holy God of the universe, we cannot do anything we want or act unkindly and still think we are being Christian. God has called us to a higher way, a higher lifestyle. We are to follow in his steps.

Encountering the Power of God

Notice finally that in both of these stories, Balaam and the disciples are met by the presence of God. When one reads in the Old Testament the expression "the angel of the Lord," it is not referring to God's helpers. This is a reference to the presence of God himself. When Balaam was confronted by the "angel of the Lord," it means he experienced God himself. Yahweh God confronted him and challenged him. When the disciples were walking on the road to Emmaus, their eyes were not opened until the invited guest, Jesus, broke bread, blessed it, and handed it to them, and then they saw that this unknown companion had been the Lord himself.

Sometimes in the narrow places of life, we shall experience the presence of God. The angel of God will come and minister to us. Sometimes he may come to you in the narrow place of grief, illness, pain, or suffering. He may come to you in the narrow place of rejection, ridicule, loneliness, and depression. He may come to minister to your need and lift you up. God may come to you speaking through a friend, a telephone call, a note, or a letter. He may come to you in many places and ways and communicate his presence to you as power, grace, and love. In the narrow places of life, God is there. Let him open your eyes.

One of the messages that comes to us from the Emmaus passage about Jesus, however, is that God is not always just at our disposal. After he revealed himself, he disappeared. They met him in the word and in the fellowship at the table, but God is not somebody we can manipulate with little schemes and systems. We cannot memorize a few things that will automatically produce God for us. God is not on a string for our use. He is not simply available at our whim. He may surprise us by the manner of his coming, but we do not control or manipulate him. He is the God who comes at his own beckoning. He is the God who moves in our lives in his own way, and we must be open to his coming in unexpected places and in unexpected ways. We need the miracle of the "opened eyes" and "the burning heart."

The Better End

Paul Scherer, that hurricane of a preacher, wrote in one of his books about a misrepresentation of a phrase that he stumbled across.[2] Often, he said, we talk about seeing something through until "the bitter end." In some research he did on that phrase, he discovered that originally it was not "the bitter end" but "the better end." This phrase came from the time when a ship was caught in a storm and the anchors were let down into the water, and then the ship would move out to the end of the cables that reached deep into the hull of the ship. "The better end" was secured far within the hull of the ship, and when the storms came, the ship could ride them out because the better end was secured.

Too many of us try to live out life to "the bitter end," when the alternative is to let God be with us to "the better end," which is the end where his presence is. At the better end, he will sustain us. God may first come to meet us in judgment. We may sense him in narrow places and in unexpected ways, and his coming may even surprise us with his presence. Come he will. Be assured of that. We cannot control his means or time. I hope that you and I will not give way to the bitter end but that we learn instead to embrace the better end where the presence of God will sustain us and carry us through.

11

Isaiah: Finding It Hard to Wait

Isaiah 40:27-31

Much of our life is spent waiting. If we do not learn how to live while we wait, we will likely miss much of life. A friend of mine muses, "A lot of living is spent in the meantime." It has never been easy for people to wait in any age. But a flashing sign of our adolescence today is our glaring inability to wait. We are an age of impatience. We want what we want immediately. We want instant gratification. We want results on demand and actions when requested. We want immediate news from overseas and even from astronauts in outer space. And often we get it that way by television or the internet. Many today prefer instant tea or instant coffee and minute steaks. They want frozen food made available instantly. Microwaves cook our meals much faster than old-fashioned ovens. We have instant copy makers and fax machines, and many have smart phones, emails, and texts to communicate quickly. We have many gadgets and machines to get results quickly or to satisfy our needs immediately. Our lifestyle is one of impatience. We want to be satisfied right now.

Waiting Is a Part of Life

Yet I wonder how realistic that is or has ever been. I recall that as a boy I spent a lot of time waiting. I remember waiting to go to kindergarten and then waiting until I was old enough to go to first grade. I remember waiting for the school bus. I remember waiting for Saturday so I could go to the old Trenton Theatre and see the "shoot-'em-up" movie. I remember waiting for Christmas Day to arrive, then waiting to go to my grandmother's house for a meal with our extended family, and then waiting to get back home to play with my toys. I recall waiting to go to high school, waiting to go to college, and waiting to go to seminary. Later I remember waiting to get married, waiting for my first child, waiting for my second child, and later waiting for my grandchildren.

Much of life is spent waiting. Think about your own life. How much of your life do you spend simply waiting? Reflect on the time you spend waiting at the grocery or department store or waiting at the doctor's or dentist's office. Time is spent waiting for a telephone call from that certain guy or girl, waiting for a call, text, or email from overseas or across the country from a friend or relative, or waiting for the bell to ring at school. "Will this class never end?" you ask yourself. You spend time waiting to go home for Christmas, waiting to get your grades, waiting to graduate, waiting for a job, waiting for somebody else to meet you, waiting for piano lessons to end, waiting for the baby to arrive, waiting for the plane, waiting for the game, play, or concert to begin. We are busy waiting for something. But most of us are not good at waiting.

J. Barrie Shepherd said that when he was a small boy his father owned a bakery shop. His father would knead dough, getting it ready to make the morning rolls. After the dough reached the right consistency, he would drop it in an enormous barrel and then place a piece of yeast on top of the dough and go to bed. Then he would have to get up early the next day before dawn. The fresh, light dough would have risen to the top of the barrel. He said that the rolls his father made from that dough were absolutely delicious. Then America invented a new instant rising substance called "flying dough." His father could sleep later in the morning and prepare the rolls the night before, but Shepherd said that the rolls were never the same again.

Now let me tell you a secret. If you have never tasted a roll made from scratch, or a cake baked from scratch, or a biscuit made from scratch, you haven't really lived! I have been especially blessed to have a wife who can make rolls, cakes, and biscuits from scratch. The others that come from a can, the frozen department, or a prepackaged container are not the real things. But that is a part of the sacrifice we make to have everything ready instantly. Convenience or impatience sometimes may cause us to give up some of the better things of life.

The Frustration of Waiting

The prophet Deutero-Isaiah[1] knew something about the problem of waiting. He was speaking to a people who had been waiting for fifty years to be delivered from their captivity in Babylon. But they had heard no word from God. They longed to go back home to Israel. They wondered where God was. Our text notes first that the children of Israel were filled with frustration and anxiety. They had become faint and weary from waiting. Their long-term burden of suffering and enslavement had affected their mental attitude, and they were disappointed and depressed. Our bodily condition often affects our attitude. They had been demoralized from their long years of being away from home in captivity in a foreign land. God's way seemed hidden from them. They cried out and asked, "Where is God? Why doesn't God do something?" They were not concerned whether God was up in the sky or in the stars, but they wanted to know if God was near them in their time of need. They wanted to know if God could do anything to help them in their plight. "Does God care about us?" they asked. In their emotional fatigue and depression, they cried out to God. They were suffering from frustration and anxiety and in the depths of self-pity.

You and I understand those kinds of feelings. There are times when our emotions overcome us because we are weary and faint from physical and mental burdens. Like Israel in Isaiah's day, we want to know where God is. I visited a woman recently who told me she had just talked with her doctor. "I am so tired of hearing him say, 'At your age you have to expect some of your parts to wear out.'" "Why?" she asked. "Why is life that way?" Her body had an effect on her emotions, and depression had sunk in. Our bodies and feelings are tied together. Many of us are frustrated and weary with waiting for something to happen. We have some dream, goal, hope, desire, or ideal that we long to realize. But it has not come to pass. Our hope has not been realized or our dream may be unfulfilled, and so we soon become depressed and hit bottom. We feel hopeless or trapped. And we ask, "Is there any word from God?"

The Call for Patience

Second, Isaiah was aware of Israel's frustration and anxiety, but note that he encouraged the people to learn to be patient where they were. Even in their waiting, he reminded them that God was present with them. "God is working in ways beyond your understanding," Isaiah informed them (v. 28). While they waited, God wanted them to learn to live in the meantime. To a degree, they had done this. They had married, built houses, and had families. They had planted crops and carried on with life as best they could while living in captivity. While they waited to return to Israel, they lived in the meantime.

The Gospels record people waiting centuries for Christ to come. We read about Elizabeth waiting to give birth to her son. Simeon and Anna waited to see the anointed One before they died. Mary and Joseph waited for the birth of Jesus. They all waited with expectation and hope. But that did not mean that their wait was easy. In the Christmas season, we too look again for signs of the coming Christ. We wait to celebrate his birth again. Harold Kohn, a minister and naturalist, said that man/woman is the only creature who has learned much about how to wait. When the amoeba encounters its food, it doesn't wait; it just consumes it. If you want to teach a dog or a cat to wait before they eat, you have a real job on your hands to train them not to eat their food when it is placed before them. If they have no training, there is immediate consumption. And the same is true with many animals in their mating process. There is little wooing, only instantaneous gratification. But man/woman knows something about wooing and courting and the ability to wait. We plant crops because we have learned to wait for the harvest. We learn how to wait. But not many of us have learned how to wait effectively.

Waiting requires a great deal of patience. Someone once criticized Leonardo da Vinci because he would stand looking at his mural of *The Lord's Supper* for hours before he would apply a single stroke. People could not understand why he would spend so much time just standing there and looking. He responded by saying, "My most telling strokes come after the longest pauses." His greatest creativity came from his ability to wait until his stroke was clear to him. The best parents, the best teachers, are those who know something about patience. Parents and teachers give guidance and knowledge and then wait for the child to absorb it. Education requires the ability to wait and see somebody blossom, develop, grow, and mature. We guide and instruct and then need the ability simply to wait.

Medical doctors have learned to cooperate with waiting. A doctor may remove a tumor or perform surgery and then, when that part is over, the process of healing must take place. Healing requires waiting. Healing takes time. Healing works on its own. The doctors have done their work. Now time and waiting must take place before their work is complete. Paul reminds us that creation itself is not finished. It is still in the process of waiting to be completed. Nature itself waits for its final goal (Rom 8:20-21).

Some years ago, I lost fifty percent of the hearing in one of my ears from a viral infection, and my doctor gave me a prescription of rest. He said I needed to wait and let my body's natural defenses work on the infection to bring healing. "What kind of prescription was that?" I thought. "I want some medicine. Give me something to get rid of this problem." But the doctor's prescription was to wait. Wait! That was not and is not an easy prescription for any of us to take. Waiting can be a hard pill to swallow.

In one comic, the cartoon characters Charlie Brown and Lucy are talking. Lucy says to Charlie Brown, "Do you know how many great moments in your life you have wasted? Here comes a great moment right now. This is the moment. Bang, it's gone. It's wasted. And you didn't do a thing with it." Charlie Brown says, "You are not much fun to have around." Anybody who wants to tell us to live creatively is not somebody we usually want to have around. Nevertheless, we may often need some buzzing bee to remind us to live in the present and stop wasting some of the most precious moments by waiting to live later. We need to learn to live in the time while we wait.

The Anticipation of Something Better

Third, notice that one of the reasons Israel may not have been able to live effectively where they were was that they kept anticipating going home. They continued to anticipate something better, something beyond, and returning to something that they did not have. That kind of anticipation is good and bad. Many of us are not able to learn to live right in the meantime because we keep looking down the road. You have heard people say, "Well, if only my wife were different." Or "If only my husband saw things differently." Or "If only I had different circumstances." Or "If only I could live differently or live in another place." So we live in the future and wait for tomorrow. We look to another place and time or when we graduate or get another job or have more money or the children leave home.

When I have ministered to people who had heart attacks or bouts with cancer or some other serious illness that threatened their lives, they have almost universally told me about the reordering of priorities. They are no longer looking way down the road. They begin to look more seriously at the present moment. The meantime has become more sacred. Now they ask, "What can I do with the gift of this moment? How can I best live now?" Too many of us look down the road into the future and seek to find life's meaning in a distant direction instead of living in the present.

Wait with Hope

The writer of our Scripture text offers us a fourth lesson. Isaiah says we have to learn to wait with hope. Waiting can teach us lessons about hope. We can wait or we can wait with hope. We wait with hope in the awareness that the Creator God leads us in ways beyond our ability to understand or grasp. This everlasting God never grows weary or faint. The Apostle Paul writing in the epistle to the Romans reminds us that we wait not as those who have no hope. We wait with expectation (Rom 8:24-25). We do not wait for the end to come with inevitability. It will not arrive with a boom and end in despair. We wait with eager anticipation and hope, because we have the assurance that God is in charge of the end of time.

In England the Christmas carolers who used to come by homes singing were called "Waits." The "Waits" shared the Christmas message through music. While we are living in the time of waiting, we need to learn to sing the song of hope. Waiting can teach the Christian how to sing. The Christian cannot be caught up in the despair of the moment, whether there is illness or surgery or sickness or whatever the world conditions are, because we know we wait not without hope but with a sense of the power and presence of God in our lives to sustain us.

We have experienced his love in Christ, and we know that God loves us and cares for us. We wait in expectation that God will come to meet our need and strengthen us. We wait for God to come anew in our lives especially in the Christmas season. In a world filled with so much darkness, disease, war, poverty, and injustice, we need to sing songs again of hope, love, peace, joy, forgiveness, and grace. We do not need more prophets of gloom and doom, but those who will deliver songs of encouragement and the possibilities of new beginnings. As Christians, we need to light candles of hope in a world filled with too much darkness.

God Is Constant

A fifth lesson from our text today is about trust. Isaiah reminds the people of God's faithfulness and constancy. God is from everlasting to everlasting. God is not a God who grows weary or faint. God is present even when we are weary, tired, depressed, and beaten down by difficult circumstances or events. God is ever present. "Have you not known, have you not heard?" Isaiah asked Israel. Have you not known what kind of God we worship? We sometimes assume that faith precedes knowledge. Paul stated, "I know whom I have believed." But sometimes knowledge about God precedes faith. Isaiah reminded Israel of that here. He was reminding them of some great truths about God to help them recall or stimulate their faith. Their concept of God was too small. Remember that the Lord is an everlasting God. God is the creator of the world. We can never understand the greatness of God or fathom God's understanding.

The basic meaning of the word "wait" comes from the root Hebrew word *qavah*, which means "to wind or twist" like a rope or the fibers in a spider's web. "To wait upon the Lord" is to let God become your lifeline, to let God be your cord of escape and to find your strength in God. This concept of "waiting" is not passively doing nothing. It is waiting eagerly like a farmer who waits for crops from seeds he has planted. It is waiting linked with our faith in God, knowing that no matter what our troubles or difficulties are, God is always present to sustain us.

Have you ever read or heard how an eagle builds her nest? The eagle makes a nest first with thorns and then places wool or other soft items over the thorns. Then the eagle lays her eggs. When the small eaglets are hatched, they live in the soft nest and are fed for a while. When it is time for the little eagles to fly, the old eagle removes the soft wool from her nest with her talons and exposes the sharp thorns to the eaglets. The nest is uncomfortable and pricks them. They have to fly out of the nest because the thorns cut them. The young eaglets fly with weak wings at first. The giant eagle comes under the eaglets and lets the small birds land on her wings, bearing them up and helping them fly. When the thorns of troubles, difficulties, and burdens seem to pierce us, that doesn't mean God is not present. God is with us and is seeking to bear us up under the wings of divine grace. We lean on God knowing that we can feel God's presence and power in our weakness. God will bear us up.

Strength to Endure

Last, our text reminds us about endurance. Isaiah states that we will "renew our strength" when we wait on God. The words "renew your strength" are more accurately translated to say that we will find "an unfailing strength or resource from God." We will find a strong resource that reaches beyond our resources and strength. This renewal comes from God's strength, not our own. Here is a new kind of strength. It is from God. This strength will give us the power to endure. Paul reminds us, "If we hope for something we do not yet see, then, in waiting for it, we show our endurance" (Rom 8:25).

Isaiah depicts a graduated faith or a progression of faith. We are not always at the same stage in our faith. Sometimes we have faith like wings. By faith, we can lift ourselves up and fly to great heights. Many of the children of Israel wanted those wings to help them fly away and escape their bondage. Faith on this level gives us elevation and vision. At other times, by faith we are running. We may be running to avoid our difficulties and trials, running to sustain ourselves in the stresses and strains of living. But most of the time we are walking by faith. This is the faith of our ordinary days, regular rounds, and the steady pace of simply enduring. Much of life is plodding, not running or flying. The greatest work may be done in ordinary, routine ways by teachers, doctors, lawyers, carpenters, secretaries, store clerks, farmers, and millions of folks. This is the steady pace of individuals who work faithfully at their routine task again and again, day after day. In our daily work, we walk by faith that God is ever present with us.

In the Advent/Christmas season, let me encourage you again to learn how to wait. I know we don't want to do that. We think actions are always the answer and waiting is a weakness. Action seems stronger. But actions may not be the answer. We sometimes say, "Leave waiting to monks, weaklings, and mystics. Give me action." But is it not possible that the greatest source of strength may come to us in waiting? "There is a time to wait and a time to act." Knowing the right moment, discerning the time, is not always easy. But try we must.

So then, do not give way to despair, difficulties, depression, or whatever those low moments bear. Wait with hope and confidence because you know that God is present to bear you up. In this Advent season, that is the good news. There is good news of great joy. God has come into the world and we have seen his love. As we wait to celebrate Christmas again, remember that God loves you, sustains you, and will never abandon you. The birth of Jesus Christ reminds us that God loves us and is present to us in a special way.

Years ago when our children were preschoolers, we used to drive to church past a manger scene on a church lawn. Each Sunday our children would comment on that manger scene. It was a typical manger scene with shepherds, angels, and the small manger with the Christ child in it. The scene was on the lawn of another church. After Christmas was over, we drove past the church one day and our son, Bill, looked up and said, "They have put the Lord Jesus away until next Christmas."

Some of us have already placed the Christmas decorations on the tree and are getting ready for Christmas. After Christmas is over, we will put them away for next Christmas having never experienced the Christ of Christmas at all. Let us wait for God's presence to come. Let us wait with the sense of the power of God's coming and with the assurance that in our waiting God is present. We wait with assurance and hope that God has come and is coming anew within our lives to draw us closer to God's self. May your Christmas expectation be fulfilled in the strong sense of the presence of Christ. May the Lord Jesus not be put away for another year but be a present reality with each of us each day of the new year.

Sometimes at Christmas we can come aglow with the wonder of Christ, but then during the rest of the year we don't seem to sense much excitement about our faith. My prayer for you and for me in this Christmas season is that we will learn to wait for God and in our waiting sense God's presence sustaining us. It's hard to wait. But remember to bind yourself to God. In that kind of waiting, you find real strength.

Ruth: The Bond of Loyalty

Ruth 1:8-19

The book of Ruth comes as a fresh breeze in desert heat after the wars and bloody violence of Joshua and Judges. This gentle story seems like a spring flower blooming in a snow-covered field. It almost seems out of place in the midst of some of the rugged Old Testament books, and maybe that is one of the reasons it has always been so loved. The book of Ruth is a simple story, a superb example of an ancient short story or a novella—a short novel—that relates a tale of loyalty, love, and struggle. There is none of the violence in this story that is depicted in so many of the earlier Old Testament stories. The story of Ruth, "the gleaner maid," was told repeatedly through the ages by master storytellers. Drawing on oral tradition, some unknown writer put the story in the permanent form we have today. The Hebrews placed this book in the Kethubim or Writings. Its position in the writings and internal evidence indicate that the book as we have it was written after the exile.

A Hebrew Epic

The unknown author of Ruth has written a story that many regard as the finest example of the epics and idylls of the Hebrews. In a simple story that takes place in six brief scenes, the storyteller relates the tale of the Moabite heroine and her devotion to Naomi, their return to Bethlehem, their search for food and security, Ruth's marriage to Boaz, and the birth of their son, who was the ancestor of King David.

Our story opens long ago in the time of the Judges. There was a famine in the land. Elimelech and his wife Naomi left Bethlehem with their two sons for Moab, where they had been told they could find food for their family. They believed they would die if they remained in Bethlehem where the famine was severe. So they packed up everything and left for this foreign country, which for strict Jews was a difficult decision. Later their two sons married Moabite women. You can imagine the family discussions that took place before these weddings. A strict Jewish man didn't marry a Moabite woman. But these two did. After all, they were living in a foreign land and did not know if they would ever return home. This was home to them now. They needed companionship and to make their own homes.

The Death of Naomi's Husband

Then the story took a sad turn. Naomi's husband died, and shortly after his death both of their sons died. Naomi was now a widow, and with the death of her two sons, both of her daughters-in-law were widows as well. Naomi was in this foreign land without a husband or a son to care for her. This was the day and age when it was a man's world. Without a husband or a son to care for her, a woman was in a sad situation.

Naomi finally decided that she could no longer remain in Moab. There was no future for her there, and it was safe to return to Bethlehem. She offered her daughters-in-law an opportunity to go with her or to remain in Moab. After they traveled a short distance and then came to a fork in the road, Naomi reminded both Ruth and Orpah again, "You do not have to go with me. Do you know what it is going to be like when you go with me to Bethlehem? You are foreigners. You are going to be the victims of prejudice, and it is unlikely that you will ever be able to find a Jewish man who will want to marry you. You will be childless forever." At this point, Orpah decided that she would remain in Moab. She loved Naomi. She embraced her but went back home. But Ruth affirmed her allegiance and loyalty to her mother-in-law. Ruth's famous speech to Naomi has often been selected by many young couples to be a part of their marriage ceremony. This has always been humorous to me, because this is not a vow between a man and a woman. This is a pledge that Ruth is made to her mother-in-law! She made a pledge of absolute loyalty to her. Naomi had tried to set her free. But instead of freedom, Ruth chose loyalty.

Ruth's Sense of Loyalty

To me, Ruth's decision is fascinating. She chose to be loyal to a woman, her mother-in-law. Here in the book of Ruth is one of the most affirming statements for a mother-in-law that can be found anywhere. Phyllis Trible, an Old Testament scholar, is convinced that there is no more radical commitment found in the Old Testament than this one.[1] Ruth's commitment to Naomi was far more radical than Abraham's commitment to follow his divine call. He had several things that Ruth did not have. Abraham had a sense of his calling. He was also a man with a wife, children, servants, and many possessions. He likewise had the assurance that God would bless him. When Ruth made her commitment to Naomi, she made a commitment to a woman, a friend, in a man's world. She had not had a call from God. She had no sense of divine blessing or protection. She had no assurance of anything. Nevertheless, she made this pledge of loyalty to her mother-in-law. Her stand was a radical commitment in the day and age in which a woman's life was fulfilled through a man. Not to have a child was a disgrace for a woman. A part of Naomi's grief was the fact that she no longer had sons to carry on her name.

Listen to the radical commitment Ruth made to Naomi: "Wherever you go, I will go. Any place you choose as home will be mine—not just here in Moab, my homeland, but wherever you go." Ruth turned her back on her home and went with Naomi. "Wherever you lodge, I will lodge." It didn't have to be a mansion or a luxurious abode. Wherever Naomi went, wherever she stayed, Ruth said, "I will be there with you. Your people will be my people." The Israel that she knew only through Naomi would be Ruth's adopted country. "Your God will be my God." She turned her back on her own religion and chose the religion of Naomi. "Where you die, I will choose to die." This was a journey without thought of returning to her homeland. "I will be buried in the same place where you will be buried." This family burial acknowledges family kinship.

Ruth then made a radical commitment to go with Naomi to Bethlehem. If you want to use this statement in a wedding ceremony, remember that it was originally a pledge to a mother-in-law. You, of course, can adapt it and make it have a special place in your wedding service. But remember what a radical commitment you are making to the one you love.

As I read these words of loyalty that Ruth said to Naomi, I wondered what has happened to that kind of loyalty today. There seems to be an absence of loyalty in our marriages, businesses, churches, and other places. Where are the people who will stand by us no matter what happens? Is that loyalty evident in the behavior of husband, wife, children, parents, or the loving community of the church? Loyalty is one of the solid rocks in Ruth's life and forms a vital part in the meaning of this story.

Returning Home

The two women walked down the streets of dusty Bethlehem. They staggered under the weight of the load they had carried from Moab and sat down by the village well to rest and get a drink of water. One of the villagers at the well looked at the women and asked, "I know you, don't I? Aren't you Naomi? Didn't you use to live here?" "Don't call me Naomi, meaning pleasant, any longer," Naomi said. "Call me Mara, which means bitter. God has turned his hand away from me. My husband and my sons are dead." "Oh, we are so sorry," the woman said. "We didn't know."

Naomi and Ruth searched for what was once the house of Elimelech. When they finally found it, they saw that it lay in ruins. Naomi had been gone a long time. They made a place in the ruins where they could spend the night. Naomi discussed with Ruth what they would try to do as two poor, desperate women. The only option Naomi felt they had was to gather any barley that might be left in the fields as it was being harvested. It was the custom in Israel in that day for an owner not to harvest the grain in the corners of his field. The corners and whatever else they missed were left to be gathered by poor people, so they could get enough grain to make bread and eat.

The Field of Boaz

Ruth went out searching for a field where she might find some grain. By chance, the story tells us, she went to the field of Boaz. She began to gather some leftover grain. Boaz noticed this young woman and asked his servants, "Who is this?" They informed him that she was the daughter-in-law of Naomi, his cousin. He instructed his servants not only to let her gather the leftover grain but also to drop some so she could have plenty. He encouraged his servants to protect her and keep him informed about her needs. One day Boaz passed where Ruth was working and asked her if he could share his lunch with her. Thus began their love story.

Happily, Ruth disclosed to Naomi that she had met Boaz, the owner of the fields where she had been gleaning. Naomi's eyes lit up. This woman, who had to survive in a man's world, suddenly realized that maybe there was an avenue out of their poverty. This short story is called "Ruth," but the real hero is Naomi. The story begins with Naomi in Moab and ends with Naomi holding her grandchild. She is the one who is always working behind the scenes to bring about what needs to be done.

Wheels turned in her head as she heard about Boaz. "You are not familiar with this, Ruth," Naomi said, "but in our Jewish tradition there is a custom called 'levirate marriage.' According to this custom, if a man dies without children, his brother's duty is to marry the widow and have children and bring them up not as his own but as his brother's and they would inherit his property. Mahlon, your husband, does not have a brother who is alive. He died, as you know. But Boaz is a kinsman. He is a cousin. He is a compassionate man and follows the law strictly. So maybe we can persuade him to marry you."

Naomi's Plan

"Let me tell you about a plan I have in mind," Naomi continued. "Tonight, after Boaz is asleep, go visit him. You dress in your finest clothes, and when he falls asleep, go into his room and lie across his feet." The phrase "uncover the feet" is a euphemism for uncovering the genitalia. "When he awakens, you tell him that you have come to ask him to be your kinsman redeemer. This is our Jewish way of asking him to marry you and to do the right thing as your kinsman." "What?" Ruth responded. "I can't do that! Only prostitutes go running around at night into houses of men who are not their husbands. What would Boaz think?" "Listen," Naomi said, "we are desperate women. You can't go around thinking merely of your reputation. You have to think of having children, and this man can possibly be your husband. Let's use this desperate method to see whether he will do the right thing." Ruth conceded, "Well, I'll try."

Kinsman Redeemer

Night soon fell. Boaz had worked hard all day and likely had drunk heavily before falling asleep. He was awakened in the night to discover someone at his feet. Startled, he asked, "Who is there?" "It is Ruth," the young woman replied, "and I have come to ask you to spread your garment over me." This is a Jewish metaphor that is a way of asking someone to marry you. "I want you to be my kinsman redeemer," Ruth said. Boaz quickly agreed to accept this responsibility. After all, he was an old man, thirty-five years old! Here was this young woman, probably seventeen, who was attracted to him. It sounded like a good deal to this "old" man, who had been a bachelor a long time. None of the young women seemed to want him. So Ruth would not be disgraced, Boaz had her leave slightly before dawn so nobody would see her. He gave her a sign of his promise by filling her veil with grain to take back to Naomi. This was a sign that he would be faithful and do the right thing.

However, Boaz knew there was a problem. He wasn't the closest relative to Ruth's first husband. One other cousin was a closer relation than he was. But Boaz was a rich and important man in the city. He called ten elders to the city gate and asked his cousin to come about a matter of business. "Your cousin Mahlon's land is for sale," he said. "I would like to buy it, but you have first right to it." The cousin said, "You know, I think I might want to buy that land." "There is one hitch," Boaz noted. "If you want the land, you must marry Ruth, the Moabite, and then you have to raise her children as Mahlon's children." "Now wait a minute," the cousin said. "I am not interested in that. I am already married, and I have my children and I don't want to have children for somebody else. You can have the land. I am taking off my shoe as a sign that the deal is settled." So it was done.

Boaz went back and informed Ruth and Naomi, "I can be your kinsman redeemer." Boaz and Ruth got married, and, as we see in the final scene of the story, a child was born named Obed. Obed was the father of Jesse, who was the father of David, who was the great-great-great-grandfather, according to Matthew's genealogy, of Jesus our Lord. Ruth's child was brought in and placed on Naomi's breast, as though it were her child as well. The story concludes with a picture of Naomi, who now has a child through her daughter-in-law. Naomi had worked quietly behind the scenes to bring about this event. The story ends with the lives of Naomi, Ruth, and Boaz being filled with joy and happiness because of the birth of this child.

God in the Shadows

The Book of Ruth doesn't speak a great deal about God. But God is the chief actor. However, God remains hidden in the shadows. God is in the background. The master storyteller does not say that God always answers the prayers of Naomi. Naomi prays but God does not answer. The writer states that Ruth came "by chance" into the field of Boaz. In Hebrew, *panim* is a plural word that acknowledges that both God and humans have multiple "faces," depending on the context. God is behind all of what appears to be chance or coincidence. God works in the shadows and in the background to bring about his will. He works through this foreigner to teach tolerance. He works through Naomi's cousin, Boaz, to teach the people faithfulness and loving-kindness toward each other. God's providence is unmistakable. Divine intentionality, not luck, guides the human path.

God's providence may often be hidden to human eyes. God seems to me to work that way in my own family. Hasn't that been true for you? I don't know about you, but I never got a special text from God in which he said that this is exactly how I was supposed to rear my children or how I was to act as a father or husband. I have often wished I had received that kind of clear-cut advice. There were important times when I felt I needed a text or a vocal word. But I have sensed that God seems to work more in the background, through other people, and through his church as he makes his way and will known.

The Face of God

Several years ago, I was at a conference in Chicago, and a woman at this meeting told about an experience she had in the kindergarten where she was a teacher. She asked the children in her class to color some pictures. She gave them crayons, and they were busy at the task. One small child took his crayon and colored his page completely yellow. The teacher asked the child, "What is your picture?" He looked up at her and said, "Why, this is a picture of God" "A picture of God?" she asked. "Yes, it is a picture of God," the child responded. Then before she thought, the teacher said, "But no one knows what God looks like." The child thought for a moment and then responded, "Well, after they see my picture, they will!"

Part of the purpose of the story of Ruth and many of the other biblical stories, it seems to me, is that we might see the face of God. The "face of God" is revealed through the lives of countless men and women who have loved and served God. Supremely, we have seen the "face of God" in Jesus Christ.

This story doesn't tell us that Ruth was a beautiful woman. Suppose she had been ugly. Suppose Boaz was sixty-five or seventy. Would that change the story? It would still tell us about love, loyalty, and care, and how the providence of God worked through the lives of people. The face of God is seen in people like Naomi, Ruth, and Boaz. But we see the face of God supremely in Jesus Christ, our Lord. May his image be forever manifest in our lives and in our homes.

Some major themes or lessons arise from this book. Let me address a few.

The Providence of God

The first lesson focuses on the providence of God. Although God is not mentioned in the book of Ruth, God's presence is depicted in the shadows. God's providence is evident not in direct ways but in more elusive ways, such as when Ruth "happened to come to the part of the field belonging to Boaz." Naomi said to Ruth, "Wait . . . until you learn how the matter turns out." After the birth of Obed to Ruth, the women affirmed their recognition of the guiding presence of God when they declared, "Blessed be the LORD." God's providence might be hidden to human eyes, but the author believed that God directs all the events of one's life. It is the divine intention of God and not luck that directs the human path. "The book of Ruth presents God's working as hidden and mysterious," Katharine Doob Sakenfeld declares, "like yeast at work in a loaf of bread, until all is transformed."[2] "There is in this story," Eric Rust asserts, "a striking illustration of how God raises the humble and uses the weak things of this world for his glory."[3]

Acceptance of Foreigners

Second, the book supports the tolerance and acceptance of foreigners. Ruth addresses the exclusive practices of those who did not want to permit mixed marriages of foreigners to Israelites for fear that they would corrupt the Jewish faith. The author argues that Ruth the Moabitess, a foreigner, could be assimilated into the religious life of the Jewish people and make an essential contribution. The genealogy at the conclusion of the book, where David is listed as a descendant of Ruth the Moabitess, highlights the fruitfulness of intermarriage.

A Strong Friendship

A third lesson in the book is seen in the strong friendship between Ruth and Naomi. Even the marriage of Ruth to Boaz was subordinated to these women's trust and commitment to each other. Although the book is titled "Ruth," the story begins and concludes with Naomi. Ruth's words, "Entreat me not to leave you," were a radical commitment to her friend Naomi. Ruth the Moabitess chose Naomi the Judahite, her mother-in-law, as the one through whom she would receive direction and guidance. Ruth chose to turn her back on her own country, her familiar world, and her religion when she decided to go with Naomi.

Loving-kindness

A fourth significant lesson in the book is found in the word translated from the Hebrew as "kindness," "loving-kindness," "steadfast love," "covenant faithfulness," or "covenant loyalty." This "steadfast love" is seen in Ruth's devotion to Naomi. It is displayed in Boaz's kind treatment of Ruth as she gleans in the field and in their encounter at the threshing floor. It is evidenced in Boaz's response to be the "kinsman redeemer" for Ruth. Throughout the story, one is able to discern the power of "loving-kindness" in the lives of all the characters. Ruth, Naomi, Boaz, and even Orpah interact with each other with a high sense of values. This view of "loving-kindness" is depicted as more than just human "kindness" or "loyalty"; it is patterned after the undeserved love that we receive from God.

Covenant

The fifth lesson in the book, I believe, is related to covenant. The word "covenant" does not occur in the story, but the concept is present. Naomi's complaint and bitterness suggest that she felt that the God of the covenant had let her down. The story draws the concept of covenant even to a day-to-day contact with other people and the responsibility of each covenant believer for another. The covenant community shared in one another's lives, as evidenced in the scene at the city gate (4:7-11). Boaz fulfilled his role of "kinsman redeemer" as a part of the covenant community. Ruth's loyalty and fidelity and the kindness of Boaz were signs of the intertwining of the human and divine aspects of the covenant. Naomi found her security through human deeds, yet words such as "to cleave to" (1:14) and "not abandoning" (1:16) are covenant expressions. We can see the work of the covenant God, who directs the action from behind the scenes.

The concept of levirate marriage needs some explanation for today's congregation. According to this custom, a brother-in-law would marry his brother's widow and raise up children for his dead brother so that his name and line might continue. (See Gen 38 and Deut 25:5-10.) Boaz was not a brother but a kinsman of the deceased sons of Naomi. In the threshing floor scene, Ruth said to Boaz, "Spread your skirt over your maidservant." This phrase "spread your wing" or "cover with your skirt" was a common Near Eastern expression symbolizing protection and marriage.

The threshing floor scene may shock some of us today when we realize that the writer meant to have the readers struggle with the possibility that Boaz and Ruth might have had sexual intercourse. Ruth went, at the advice of Naomi, "prepared like a bride," and the uncovering of Boaz's legs clearly had provocative implications. But the author indicated that, when faced with this moral choice, both decided in favor of the righteous way. Ruth had shown courage in exposing herself to being treated shamefully. Boaz revealed that he too was a person of honor. He conducted himself properly and agreed to be the "kinsman redeemer."

A Radical Decision

A sixth lesson comes from the radical decision making of Ruth (Ruth 4:7-11). As I mentioned earlier, Phyllis Trible is convinced that there is no more radical decision in all the memories of Israel than the one made by Ruth. Ruth's decision, she believes, surpasses Abraham's in its radicality.[4] Abraham made his decision with a sense of divine call. He was a man with a wife and many possessions. Ruth's decision was made without a sense of call from God. She had received no promise of protection or assistance from God or any other group. She committed herself to her friend and mother-in-law, Naomi, in a man's world. This commitment had no assurance of blessing but offered instead possible hunger and death. Her decision has come to symbolize the noblest expression of human friendship. Ruth subordinated her will to a higher way of sacrificial love and service. Orpah also loved Naomi, but Ruth loved Naomi to the extent that she resolved to love Naomi's God as well.

Listen to Ruth's words to Naomi: (1) "For where you go I will go"; (2) "Where you lodge I will lodge"; (3) "Your people shall be my people"; (4) "And your God my God"; (5) "Where you die I will die."

Ruth was willing to go anywhere, without set conditions, to embrace a nation of people she had once despised, to bow before Yahweh with her religious devotion, and to be buried with Naomi wherever they might be so that even death would not separate them. As the plot unfolds and Ruth later marries Boaz and bears a son, the storyteller leads the reader from Naomi's cry of bitterness to her declaration of joy for Ruth, who is better than seven sons (4:15). Many see this story as one of the most remarkable tales of devoted friendship in the Bible.

The Image of the Kinsman Redeemer

A seventh lesson focuses on the "kinsman redeemer" image (Ruth 4:7-14). The verb "to act the part of kinsman" or "to redeem," which is applied to Boaz in this passage, is used by other Old Testament writers to depict the redemptive action of God. (See Job 19:25; Isa 43:1, 14; 44:23; Pss 78:35; 106:10.) This points to the redemptive activity of God that the New Testament expresses in the figure of Jesus Christ. The Gospel of Matthew traces the genealogy of Jesus through Ruth and Boaz (Matt 1:5). The "kinsman redeemer" was a human illustration of "loving-kindness" that pointed to a divine redeemer at work behind the scenes. In Jesus Christ, the focus of God's divine activity moved from the shadows and became visible: "And the Word became flesh and dwelt among us" (John 1:14); "In him [Jesus Christ] we have redemption through his blood, the forgiveness of our trespasses, according to the riches of his grace which he lavished upon us" (Eph 1:7).

"The story of Ruth and the story of Jesus Christ," Katharine Doob Sakenfeld notes, "invite us to have loyal kindness and to follow the God in whom dividing walls of hostility are still being broken down."[5] Let us be bridge builders and not those who construct dividing walls of hostility and prejudice.

Esther: Courageous Action

Esther 4:1-17

Along with Ruth, Esther is the other of the two brief Old Testament books that are a superb example of the ancient short story or novella. It was written not only to entertain but also to edify and inform its readers. Scholars have debated whether the book is totally historical but think it might contain a nucleus of historical truth similar to historical novels today. Every element within the story did not have to be historically accurate for the basic theme to be communicated. Esther and Ruth are both included with Song of Songs, Ecclesiastes, and Lamentations in the third Jewish division called the Ketuvim or Kethubim—Writings. The position in the Writings, along with internal evidence, suggests a late date for these books. Drawing on oral tradition that had transmitted these tales through the years, master storytellers, writing most likely after the exile, gave them their present form. Scholars project that Esther might have been written as early as the fifth century BCE, but more likely, from internal evidence, it was written in the late fourth or early third century BCE.

The Purpose of Esther

The book of Esther was probably written to explain the origin of the Feast of Purim. This festival is not mentioned in the rest of the Bible and was likely borrowed originally from either Babylonia or Persia. In Esther the festival is established to commemorate the victory of the Jews over their enemies during the time they were dispersed in Persia.

This festival is still observed today on the fourteenth and fifteenth of Adar (around March 1). It is not a religious holiday but a secular celebration filled with feasting, gaiety, and the giving of gifts.

Esther's Inclusion in the Biblical Canon

Esther has had a tumultuous time as part of the canon of Scripture. Martin Luther, along with many others, wanted to exclude it. The book is not referred to in the New Testament, and none of the church fathers wrote an exposition of it. There is no suggestion in the book that faith, prayer, or any religious factors have a role in the story's events. Lewis Bayles Paton believed that Esther was "so conspicuously lacking in religion that it should never have been included in the Canon of the Old Testament."[1] There is much in the book that is sub-Christian, especially the extreme spirit of revenge in the last chapters. But I don't think we should dismiss this book so quickly. God may be alluded to more indirectly than directly.

Esther's Story

The book opens with a description of court life in the Persian court when Ahasuerus (Xerxes II) was king. The king liked to give extravagant banquets and show off his beautiful wives. When his wife Vashti refused to be put on display for one of his banquets, he banished her, and Esther was chosen to be his queen without revealing to Ahasuerus that she was a Jew. Mordecai, her guardian, discovered a plot against the king and relayed it to Esther, who informed the king. Haman, the king's vizier, did not like Mordecai and schemed to have him killed, along with other Jews. Esther learned of this plot and prepared to trick Haman. At a second banquet, where Haman thought he would be highly honored, he was asked to declare what kind of honors should be given to one who had great favor with the king. Thinking that it was himself who was to be honored, he offered his high tributes only to discover that it was his enemy, Mordecai, who would receive them. Through Esther's entreaties to the king and the revelation of her ethnicity, Haman's plot to have the Jews killed backfired and he was hanged on the gallows he had prepared for

Mordecai. Mordecai was rewarded with many tributes and wrote the decree that saved the Jews from persecution and death. The story declares that the activities of Esther and Mordecai preserved the nation from disaster, and they were greatly rewarded.

The book of Esther clearly gives an example of what life was like for some of the Jews in exile. Although the Jews depicted in this book were not persecuted openly for their religious views, they suffered then as they have for many centuries simply for being a minority group. Esther and Mordecai were drawn as examples to show that Jews could rise to positions of success and renown even in a Gentile world. This book does not offer a plea for particular religious customs to be observed during the time of exile, but it issues a firm conviction of the indestructibility of Israel and the obligation of every Jewish person to aid in this cause no matter what the personal risk might be.

The Providence of God

In the book of Esther, God seems to be working in people's lives in a quiet, hidden way. The writer seems to be hiding God's providence. The author speaks of God in a "secular" way, and God remains in the "shadows." This kind of writing, without mentioning God, might have permitted the book to address a wider audience than if it spoke directly about God's involvement in the affairs of the characters in the story.

"God in the Shadows" could be an appropriate description of the providence of God as discerned in this novella. Several biblical texts could be noted here. The name Esther means "hidden" in Hebrew. What is hidden? Is it the presence of God? The hand of God can be observed in the "coincidences" in Esther, such as the king's insomnia and the reading of the account of Mordecai's earlier deed of saving the king's life, which had gone unrewarded (Esth 6:1-2), as well as in the whole series of events that lead to Esther's becoming queen, all of which appear to be only "secular" happenings. The most famous verse in Esther, "And who knows whether you have not come to the kingdom for such a time as this?" (4:14), could be a declaration of the hidden God without ever mentioning him. J. G. McConville, an Old Testament scholar at Trinity College in Bristol, England, declares that "the silence about God is quite deliberate, not to make the point that he is inactive in human situations, but on the contrary, that he is hidden behind all events."[2]

When we read Esther carefully, we begin to see more than mere coincidences: the king's forgetting to reward Mordecai for saving his life yet keeping a record of it and, at the "right moment," being reminded of this experience; Haman's presence in the king's court to condemn Mordecai just as the king is prepared to reward Mordecai; and the presence of the gallows in Haman's house that was constructed for Mordecai but became, ironically, the place where Haman himself was hanged. Behind these suspenseful and surprising coincidences, the writer is pointing to the providential power of God, who directs the course of events in the lives of men and women.

Although Esther does not speak much about God, God's presence does brood over the events and is the real force working behind them. Is it not a lesson of the way God continues to work out his purpose in the world today, silently and slowly through the lives of many individuals? Working behind the freedom he has given people to act, God is steadily advancing his cause even through the lives of those who do not recognize him. I know that in my own life it is easier to see the working of God in hindsight than in knowledge I had before I made a decision. Looking back on my life, I often see more clearly how God has directed my path than I did when trying to discern God's will and direction.

As we reflect on this story, we will have to seek to understand some of the difficult customs in the ancient world. We will have to reflect on the hiddenness of God and the secular expressions of communicating that knowledge. The story of Esther provides an opportunity to deal with some of the customs and moral issues raised by the actions of Esther and Mordecai, especially the killing of the Jewish people in the empire. Some of the details in this story will raise difficulties for us. Here we will have to reflect on the higher values we have perceived in the teachings of the Christian Gospels.

The Persecution of the Jews

One of the central themes of Esther is the persecution of the Jews as a minority group in Persia. The Jewish people continue to suffer from this kind of problem in many places today. We can see how this story addresses this issue and the attitude and role of the Christian church in assisting the Jews and other minority groups. In the book, Esther becomes the symbol of deliverance, and Haman is a picture of the prejudice and injustice that have often threatened the Jews. Haman used rumors and accusations to condemn the Jews, and, unfortunately, these were quickly and easily accepted without examination by the king (see Esth 3).

An Act of Courage

The most famous verse in Esther is 4:14. Mordecai had just explained the peril that faced the Jews, and then he said to Esther, "If you keep silence at such a time as this, relief and deliverance will rise for the Jews from another quarter, but you and your father's house will perish. And who knows whether you have not come to the kingdom for such a time as this?" The opportunity for courageous action lay before Esther. She may have been tempted to be silent and do nothing. This is often the path for the selfish and fearful person. When evil demands denunciation, many people often maintain a prudential silence. Expediency is the easier path; a courageous word may demand the harder path of rejection, misunderstanding, ridicule, suffering, or even death.

But Mordecai is convinced that even if Esther refuses to act, God will move in another way, through someone else, to prevent the extinction of their people. Even if one group fails in its work for God, others will be raised up to carry the work forward. God has many instruments through whom he is working. Every opportunity presents a special call for service. Behind Esther's present opportunity stands God's providential purpose. Will she be equal to the task?

Can we not sense a similar lesson for us today as we face such challenges as war, hunger, disease, racism, nuclear bombs, pollution, and injustice? Are we equal to the tasks before us? Sidnie White

Crawford, professor of Hebrew Bible at the University of Nebraska, proclaims that the book of Esther "offers a message of hope to other minorities living in majority cultures, such as African Americans in the white dominated United States." She notes further that for those "who are oppressed the book gives a message of active faith and hope in the face of threat, and to those who rule that the rights of minorities are as important as the rulers' self-interest." She also believes that the story affirms that "the greatest social rewards come through tolerance and cooperation."[3] We live in an age when bigotry and prejudice are raising their ugly heads in a vicious way, and Christians need to challenge this. When Archbishop Desmond Tutu condemned apartheid in South Africa years ago, he said something that is still an important word for today: "Why should skin color or race be any more useful as a criterion than, say, the size of one's shoes? What has the size of my nose to do with whether I am intelligent? It has no more to do with my worth as a human being than the color of my eyes."[4] Hopefully the book of Esther will help us keep our courage and denounce racism as a sin unworthy of a human being, especially one who claims to be a Christian.

The Vengeance of Esther

The vengeance of Esther, which is seen in the second slaughter in Susa (9:11-15), reminds us that the Old Testament is incomplete. Christians cannot commend the spirit of revenge that is evident in this passage. The attitude reflected in Esther might appear to be a natural reaction for a people who had experienced so much persecution and hostility from others in this society. The wanton destruction of one's enemies, however, is still on a lower level when measured by the Christian teaching to show love, justice, forgiveness, grace, and mercy. The higher revelation came in Jesus when he declared, "You have heard it was said, 'You shall love your neighbor and hate your enemy.' But I say to you, love your enemies and pray for those who persecute you" (Matt 5:43-44).

A Different Approach

I recently heard Rabbi Hal Schevitz, pastor at Or Atid Synagogue in Richmond, Virginia, state that he believes the book of Esther is similar to a Mel Brooks satirical comedy, *Blazing Saddles*, in dealing with racism. To him, the lengthy, exaggerated, wild drinking and fornicating parties and the irony throughout the book of Esther are best explained by seeing the book as satire in a comedy setting. He believes that one of the ways some people have dealt with the radical racism against the Jews in the past is to look back and make fun of those who persecuted them. The celebration of Purim with its festive and party atmosphere arises from the teaching of the book of Esther. Schevitz likes to say, tongue in cheek, that the message of Esther is "They tried to kill us. We won. Let's eat." This satirical take is a different approach to confronting the persecution depicted in the book.

A Higher Way

Cesar Chavez, who served for years as the director of the United Farm Workers, labored hard to improve conditions for migrant workers in the United States. He tells about an experience he had when he was about fourteen years old. He and his family were migrating as they usually did, trying to find enough farm work to give themselves a livable income. One day, they went into a restaurant to eat. A sign was posted that read "Whites Only." Being Mexican, they hoped they could be served. They sat down at a table. A waitress gave them a menu and went back to get the water for their table. The owner of the restaurant chastised her for seating them. He told her to throw them out or he would fire her. She had to come back to the table and tell them, "I'm sorry, I can't serve you. You have to leave." As the family got up and walked away, Cesar walked over to the owner of the restaurant. He said he could stand it no longer, and although he was only a fourteen-year-old boy, he felt he had to speak. His family called to him to come, but he said, "I have to speak up someday and it's going to be today." He went over to the boss and asked, "Why do you have to treat people like that? Any man who behaves like you do is not even a human being." The man cursed him and said, "Go on, get out of here." But he said that from that moment on, he was determined to lift his voice against the darkness of prejudice.

We may be only one small voice whispering in the dark, but that can be a beginning. Soon that voice may join with another and another and another. Your voice and mine can be raised against the prejudice, injustice, ignorance, suffering, and pain in the world to guide people out of the darkness and into the light of the way of Christ.

Booker T. Washington once said, "I will not let any man reduce my soul to the level of hatred." As Christians, we reach for a higher way. We seek to overcome evil with good. We reach out with the love of Christ in our lives and touch evil with love. Love suffers long; love bears all things; love endures all things. When the higher way is in one's life, then this kind of love literally does overcome evil. It may suffer when it challenges evil. It may be distorted, misunderstood, and abused, but love will be triumphant in the world because hate only begets hatred. Ultimately, love will win because it is the higher, better way. As the apostle Paul has reminded us, "Do not be overcome by evil but overcome evil with good" (Rom 12:21).

14

Elijah: From the Mountain to the Valley

1 Kings 18:20-29, 36-39; 19:1-2, 10-13

I find myself drawn again and again to the ninth-century BCE prophet named Elijah from Tishbe in Gilead, who clothed himself with a garment of haircloth and a leather girdle. I have found especially appealing the story of his flight into the wilderness and mountains during a low moment in his life. I have discovered that it is more than just an ancient tale, but it is my story, your story, and the story of many others. Elijah had won a great victory. He was triumphant over the prophets of Baal on Mt. Carmel. In his victory over the false prophets on that mountaintop, the manifestation of God was seen clearly by all.

Self-pity

After his great victory, Elijah received threats from the queen and fled into the wilderness. He became a different man entirely. Once he had stood before 450 prophets of Baal as the only spokesperson for God. He was victorious over them, but now he is filled with self-pity. He begins to wallow in the pits of despair and despondency. He is exhausted, tired, and wrung out. He is suffering from what is commonly called "burnout" today. A death wish rises from his lips to God: "O God, take my life. I and only I am left." His emphasis is on "only." When we get in the pits of life, we often think, "I am the only person who has suffered like this. I have been faithful to God. Why should I suffer?" "All the others," Elijah says, "have led the people of

Israel into idolatry. I alone have been faithful, and here I now sit in my despair." Like Jeremiah, he cried to God: "I sat alone." He was filled with loneliness, anxiety, and despair.

Many Feel Despair or Low Moments

Elijah, of course, has not been the only person with these kinds of problems. The Scriptures are filled with similar cries. Many of the psalms echo these feelings. One psalmist looked at some people who were wealthy, saw their wickedness, and cried out about how unfair God was: "Behold these are the wicked; always at ease, they increase in riches. All in vain have I kept my heart clean and washed my hands in innocence. For all day long, I have been stricken, and chastened every morning" (Ps 73:10-14). When the children of Israel were taken captive into Babylon, out of the depths of their self-pity they cried, "By the waters of Babylon, there we sat down and wept, when we remembered Zion. On the willows there we hung up our lyres. For these our captors required of us songs, and our tormentors for mirth, saying, 'Sing us one of the songs of Zion!' How shall we sing the LORD's song in a foreign land?" (Ps 137:1-4).

"Why does the way of the wicked prosper?" asked Jeremiah. "Why do all who are treacherous thrive? Thou plant them, and they take root; they grow and bring forth fruit; thou art near in their mouth and far from their heart" (Jer 12:1-2). Even our Lord, while hanging on the cross, cried, "My God, my God, why have you forsaken me?" Try however we might, by saying that Jesus is quoting an ancient psalm (Psalm 22) or the like, I think we have here the cry of a man who is at his lowest moment in life. "God, where are you," he asks, "as I hang here in my rejection and despair?"

Familiar Problems

You and I have also known these moments of loneliness, dejection, and self-pity. Things have not gone right at work. There are problems at home. We have moved to a new city and know no one. We are having difficulties at school. We have just put a parent in a nursing home. A parent or spouse has died. One of our children has gotten into trouble. We all know these times of difficulty and our feelings of self-pity. Sometimes those moods can become so dominant in our lives that they totally control us.

Several years ago, a cartoon appeared in a magazine that depicted a small boy holding a St. Bernard dog with a leash. The boy wanted the dog to go one way, and you could see that the dog wanted to go another. The caption read, "Let's get this straight! You are my dog. I'm not your boy!" One of the things we need to get straight in our lives is that our moods should not totally control who and what we are. Life is filled with bright days and dark days, gray days and sparkling days, hazy days and radiant days. Life is filled with all kinds of ups and downs. Who wants to let the weather or our mood dominate us?

A Popular Preacher?

Let's look further at our text. Elijah was disappointed because he thought that when he conquered the prophets of Baal on Mt. Carmel, he would become a popular preacher. After all, he had won a great victory. He showed that the other prophets were inferior. Israel was in the midst of a great drought, and King Ahab had turned to the prophets of Baal to bring rain. Elijah challenged them to a theological duel, and he was dramatically victorious. The prophets of Baal stood there, all 450 of them, in their ceremonial robes, and Elijah challenged them: "Let's see which God is more powerful, Baal or Yahweh God." The preachers who worshiped Baal cried out to their god to send his fire down and consume the sacrifice that they had placed on their altar. But he did not respond. Elijah mocked them: "Maybe your god has gone on a trip. He could be asleep." They cried louder. Still there was no response.

Elijah then asked the people to pour water on his sacrifice. "Soak it in water and this will make it impossible to catch fire easily." Water was poured over the animal on the altar until the water filled the basin around the altar's base. Then Elijah prayed that Yahweh would send fire down upon his sacrifice. God sent fire down and consumed not only the sacrifice but the whole altar. Do you suppose that Elijah thought to himself, "Man, they have got to believe that Jehovah is God and I alone am his true prophet"?

Remember that this was a barbaric age. Elijah had all the prophets of Baal put to death. Then he knelt and prayed for rain. Six times he sent his servant to go and look toward the sea to see if there were any signs of rain. Each time the servant returned and announced, "There is nothing." But the seventh time, he returned and declared, "Behold a small cloud about the size of a man's hand has arisen from the sea." Soon the skies were black with clouds, thunder and lightning filled the sky, and rain began to fall. Elijah girded his haircloth garments about him, and he ran the seventeen miles to the palace of Jezreel through the pouring rain in front of the chariot of Ahab like a conqueror.

Running for His Life

But then what happened? Did the people flock around Elijah and begin following him? No. As soon as Queen Jezebel was informed that Elijah had killed the prophets of Baal, she declared, "So may the gods do to me, and more also, if I do not make your life as the life of one of them by this time tomorrow." Elijah fled for his life. He didn't understand that people are drawn to popular religion. People bow easily at the altar of popular gods, and they usually follow those who preach a popular religion. Baal symbolized security, materialism, food, and sex. That is all many people want in a god. What more could you ask for from a god? But Yahweh God challenged his followers to find a new life, and they had to go through the wilderness to get it. He demanded justice and righteousness in their dealings with each other and especially with the poor. Jehovah did not promise his people everything they always wanted but called them to help those in need. Instead of becoming a popular preacher, Elijah found himself a fugitive and on the run for his life.

Losing His Vision of God

Elijah had lost his vision of God. He had taken his eyes off the God who had empowered him on top of Mt. Carmel and turned his eyes on himself. When he turned his eyes away from God and looked inward, his faith became weak. When he began to fear Jezebel, his fear of the Lord decreased. He truly believed, "I and I alone am left."

It is interesting that he fled to Mt. Horeb. Mt. Horeb was the place where Moses saw the burning bush. Mt. Horeb was where Moses received the commandments of God. It was on Mt. Horeb that Moses spent forty days and forty nights wrestling with the spirit of God. Was Elijah trying to go home again? Was he like a motherless child who was seeking to go back through the wilderness of his life to recapture his vision of God? He traveled through the wilderness trying to find his way home to God. In his exhausted state, he awakened to find bread and water by his side. An angel had come unexpectedly to minister to him. "Without the angel," Walter Brueggemann notes, "the story would leave us with a hopeless fugitive."[1] The bread and water represent God's way of meeting the most basic needs of Elijah. They also are a sign of God's presence and care. Elijah was fed, and he rested. He was slowly brought out of his fatigue, brokenness, despair, and fear. He got needed food, drink, and rest.

Then God asked him a question: "Elijah, what are you doing here?" Elijah responded in a self-centered way, saying, "Oh, Lord, I'm . . . I'm here because I am the only one in all of Israel who is faithful to you, and now they are trying to kill me." In this passage the writer seems to focus on various aspects of the word "life." The queen threatens Elijah's life. He flees for his life. He despairs of his life. Yet he is afraid that his life will be taken. The angel gives him food to sustain his life. And God comes to direct his life. Elijah cannot escape God's question. "Elijah, what are you doing here?"

A New Vision of God

From Elijah's encounter on the mountain comes a new vision of God. He went to the top of the mountain and experienced the force of a great wind, an earthquake, and a fire. All of these natural elements may have been symbolic of what was going on inside Elijah. They certainly seemed to be symbolic of his personality. He was at times tempestuous, fiery by nature, and pulled in many directions by his inner struggles. God seemed to reveal himself at first through the natural elements around him. God slowly drew him back to an awareness of God's presence. But ultimately, Elijah does not find God through nature. God's presence is made known as "a still, small voice," or better rendered, as "a sound of gentle stillness." Samuel Terrien has translated it "the sound of utmost silence." In a moment of absolute silence, Elijah "hears" and "sees" God. The mystery and awe of God's presence overpowers him. He had gone back home again to recapture a vision of God. In seclusion he found it.

Recapture Your Vision of God

You and I would like to recapture our vision of God, wouldn't we? Can you recall, maybe when you were a child, a teenager, or a young adult, an experience you had with God that changed your life? Can you recall a place, a church, a retreat, a quiet moment, or someplace in your home where God was strangely and warmly real to you? Maybe time has passed and that vision has faded. God has seemed distant lately, and your relationship has become routine or cold. Don't you wish you could recapture that vision? Don't you wish once again that God could be real and vital in your life? He can be! That is the glory of the gospel. An experience with God is not something reserved for the past. It is not something that only the ancient prophets had.

There is a longing within all people to see God. In the Old Testament, Moses asks God to show him his face. He is informed that he cannot look on God's face and live. But God walks beside the cleft of a rock, and the Scriptures declare that Moses "saw" the "back parts" of God (Ex 33:12-23). I don't know what that means, but it stresses a profound experience Moses had with God. Isaiah said that while he was in the temple, he "saw the LORD sitting upon a throne, high and lifted up" (Isa 6:1). Paul affirmed that he saw a light brighter than the sun and heard a voice out of the radiance calling him by name while he traveled to Damascus (Acts 26:12-18). John, on the Isle of Patmos, said that "In the midst of the seven candlesticks I saw one like unto the Son of Man" (Rev 1:13).

When did you last see or hear God? Jesus said that "the pure in heart shall see God." What does it mean to see God? In the court language of the ancient Hebrews, to see the king's face was a special honor. To see God in the biblical sense means to be ushered into his presence. This gives us a personal awareness of God. No person can see God with their visible eyes, but each of us longs to experience God, to know him, and to sense the reality of his presence. If you have had that experience before, you can have it again. Or you can have it for the first time. God is here right now. He may come into your life quietly, gently, or in a resounding, thundering fashion. Who knows? But most of the time, we will discover God in "a sound of gentle stillness."

Sherwood Eddy, in his autobiography *Eighty Adventurous Years*, told how he was a selfish and cynical student at Yale until he went to hear the evangelist Dwight L. Moody preach. Reflecting on the experience, he noted,

> Before he had finished, I saw myself as I was—no good to my college, to my country, to man, or to God. I also saw Moody as he was, an uneducated man using bad grammar, but under God shaking the continent of America as he had moved the colleges and cities of Great Britain. A great thirst sprang up in my heart. Oh for a man to rise in me, that the man I was might cease to be! That night I forgot about my "good time," I went out into the field and by a great rock I wrestled with my own selfishness and sin. That night marked a turning point in my life. God became forever real to me.[2]

Each of us longs to have a sense of the reality of God's presence to go with us into our lives. With his strong presence, we can face whatever comes, knowing that he is there to sustain us. The ancient psalmist has advised, "I wait on the LORD, my soul waits and in his word I hope; my soul waits for the LORD, more than the watchman for the morning" (Ps 13:1-6). Wait. Wait with the awareness that God is everywhere, seeking to come into your life. And it is only when you have eyes to see and ears to hear that you perceive him.

Others Serving God

Elijah thought that he was the only one serving God. "I, even I only, am left." He had lost faith in others. God told him, "Now just a minute, Elijah. So you will know better, let me tell you there are seven thousand others who are serving me down here in the valley right now. They have not bowed their knee to Baal. By the way, I want you to anoint Hazael to be king over Syria and Jehu to be king over Israel, and then cast your mantle on Elisha so he can get on with my prophetic work after you are gone."

Elijah's Departure

Elisha had prayed for a double portion of Elijah's spirit. In other words, he wanted to be his heir or successor. That prayer was granted, and he saw Elijah disappear in a whirlwind of fire. The writer has carefully used symbolic and poetic language to depict the mysterious death of Elijah. His images are rich in symbolism and elusive at the same time—a chariot of fire and a whirlwind. Elisha's response to Elijah's sudden departure was not "Where is Elijah?" but "Where is the God of Elijah?" What does this note? The emphasis is not on the prophet but on God. Too often we focus our attention on the spokesperson for God and not on God.

What had God told Elijah before he was taken up? God said, "You are not alone. There are seven thousand others who are doing my work." Remember that God's work is not dependent just on you or me. He is working through many others in his world. His spirit may lead us on what seems to us like strange tangents or twisted pathways. Nevertheless, God is at work to bring about his purpose and will.

God asked Elijah a question again: "Elijah, what are you doing here?" Can you believe it! After everything Elijah had experienced, he gave the same response that he had given before: "Well, Lord, I am here because I'm the only one who has been faithful to you. And they are trying to kill me." What did God tell him? "Get out of here," he said, "and get busy serving me! Elijah, if you have experienced my presence, then quit sitting around here wallowing in self-pity. Arise!

Go into the world and get busy meeting human needs. Anoint new kings. Appoint new prophets. Get on with my work."

The pages of the New Testament reveal that many people thought John the Baptist was Elijah. This fiery desert preacher dressed and sounded like him. Others identified Jesus with the prophet Elijah in his call for a new kingdom. The three Synoptic Gospels state that on the Mountain of Transfiguration, Moses and Elijah appeared with Jesus—Moses the great lawgiver and Elijah the great prophet. As God had commanded Elijah to get on with the work he had given him to do, so Jesus instructs his disciples to get on with the work he has commissioned us to do. "Go you into all the world," he commanded. Look at the needs of the world. Get busy helping those in need. Turn your focus not inward but outward.

Some of us spend so much time focusing on ourselves that we can't see the needs around us. Turn your eyes outward into the world. You have experienced God. You know his power. Now rise, go into the world, and serve him and not yourself, not just your own needs. Reach out to meet the needs of others who are hurting, lonely, ill, frustrated, depressed, and longing for help. Turn your eyes on God and others—not yourself.

In the ancient Roman world, when a man became a part of the Roman legion, he took an oath that was called his "sacramentum." The soldier said, "I swear to follow the eagles of Caesar wherever they fly." As a soldier in the Roman legion, he knew that this meant he might have to go to the ends of the earth to serve Rome. He might go to Caledonia, Germany, or Africa. But he made his pledge to go wherever he was asked to serve.

Jesus Christ has given to you and me our "sacramentum." He has challenged, called, and commissioned us to get up and go serve him. Enough self-pity! Arise and serve!

15

Naaman: When the Ordinary Becomes Extraordinary

2 Kings 5:1-14

Deep down inside, when we are honest, we have to admit that we often long for the dramatic. We would like to be the person who makes the headlines, who writes the best seller or popular songs. We would like to be the one who makes the last-second shot and wins the basketball game. We would like to be the one who catches the pass in the end zone and scores the winning touchdown. We would like to be the player who kicks the winning field goal. We would like to be the person who rescued the young boy who fell into the river and later saw our picture flashed on the television screen. We would like to be mother or father of the year. Some would like to be the first woman senator from our state or the first woman president of the United States. Many of our dreams or daydreams focus on the dramatic. We hunger for something spectacular. We have difficulty with being ordinary. Isn't that one of the reasons the movie *Rocky* was so popular and has had so many sequels? An ordinary person does something extraordinary by becoming the world boxing champion.

Naaman as an Example

Look at the figure Naaman from the Old Testament. This man, by many standards, was already famous. He was a great warrior and a captain in the Syrian army. He was prestigious, a man of power, position, and wealth. But . . . he was a leper. Despite all his prestige, power, and money, he suffered from the dreaded disease of leprosy, which, in biblical times, had no known cure. On one of his raids in Israel, Naaman brought back a young woman who served as a slave in their home. She heard about his dilemma and told his wife about a prophet in Israel who could cure him. Naaman traveled to Israel and first went to the king, who thought he was trying to start a fight and tore his garments.

The prophet Elisha heard about Naaman and sent for him. Before he arrived, Naaman sent gifts that conveyed something of his power and prestige. But what did Elisha do? He didn't even go out and meet him. He sent his servant and said, "Oh yes, he can be cured. Tell him to dip himself seven times in the Jordan River." How did Naaman respond to that? Did he say, "That's great!" No, he was furious. He was insulted. "Why should I dip myself in that muddy river," he exclaimed, "when we have two rivers in Damascus that are far superior to this one?" He was ready to go back home. But one of his servants said, "Master, think for a moment. If he had asked you to do some great thing, some difficult thing, you would have done it, would you not? He asked you to do a simple thing. Try it and see what happens." So Naaman went down into the river, dipped himself seven times, and was cured.

Looking for the Spectacular

Naaman almost missed the miracle, didn't he? Why? He wanted something spectacular. He anticipated an extraordinary answer to his problem. He looked for something out of the ordinary. How contemporary can a story be! Often we miss the working of God in our own lives and in the church because we are constantly looking for something spectacular, extraordinary, dramatic, or unusual. We then miss God as he is slowly, constantly at work in our lives, speaking softly and moving quietly. We don't see him or hear him. We are waiting for some big vision and do not see the flash of his presence in the lightning, the movement of his spirit in the evening breeze, and the fragrance of his grace in the flowers around us.

I heard about a man who took a vacation to Atlantic City. He had a great time during his two weeks there. When he returned home, he met a man on the street who asked, "Harry, haven't you been gone? I haven't seen you for a while." "Yes, I went to Atlantic City," he replied. "Did you go to Charlie's Fishhouse while you were up there?" "No, I didn't go there," Harry responded. "Well, if you didn't go to Charlie's Fishhouse," his friend noted, "you really haven't seen Atlantic City." Harry walked along farther and met another friend. "I haven't seen you for a while, Harry," he said. "Have you been away?" "Yes, I went to Atlantic City and had a marvelous time." "Did you go to one of those showroom auctions while you were there?" "No," Harry answered. "I didn't go there." "Well, that's really seeing Atlantic City," his friend observed. "If you haven't seen one of those auctions, you really haven't been to Atlantic City." Later Harry met another friend on the sidewalk and his friend asked, "Haven't you been away, Harry?" "Yes, I went to Atlantic City," Harry responded. "Did you ride one of those bicycles on the boardwalk while you were there?" "No, I didn't do that," Harry responded softly. "Well, if you didn't rent a bicycle while you were there, you really couldn't enjoy Atlantic City." Later Harry met yet another friend who asked him, "Haven't you been away?" "No," Harry said. "I ain't been no place, and I ain't seen nothin'!"

What was Harry's problem? Well, it is your problem and my problem. Too often we let everybody else dictate what is supposed to be fun or a good time or what we can enjoy in life. As some perceive it, unless it has been spectacular, it could not be enjoyable.

Several years ago, I went to the doctor with a kidney disorder. What was his prescription? Drink more water. What kind of prescription is that? You know what I wanted: pills, a shot, a trip to the hospital, something different. "Drink more water!" Isn't this reaction part of our problem in so many areas of life? The answer for weight loss is to eat less fatty goods and most of all to eat less. If you're tired, you should get more sleep and exercise more. The simple solutions to life are often not what we want. "Give us a great miracle!" we cry. Give us government legislation, a scientific breakthrough, or something dramatic. We do not want something simple, ordinary, and commonplace.

That attitude slips into the church, doesn't it? We think we know the answer to what our churches need. We should import a super preacher from someplace else and let him bring a revival that will cure everything. I have never been in a church yet where, pretty soon after those services, everything is not back into the ordinary routine from before. What is the solution for renewal in our churches? It will come about through the weekly and daily study, worship, openness, and response to God as his spirit works in our lives through our routine way of living.

Living with the Ordinary

Like Naaman, we often miss the presence of God because we are constantly waiting for something spectacular to happen. We have difficulty living with the commonplace. Life seems too ordinary, too routine. The longing for the spectacular makes our common, ordinary tasks seem too trivial. Cooking meals, washing dishes, taking care of children, putting out the garbage, running machinery, operating equipment, repairing cars, sawing, hammering, performing surgery, lecturing in classes, typing letters, piloting airplanes, driving a bus, laying railroad ties, and working in the shop or office are among hundreds of tasks that are ordinary and routine in the lives of many. Through ordinary jobs, people carry on life's functions.

Every Person's Labor Is Important

My father was a mail carrier who walked the same route for almost thirty years. That routine delivery enabled people along his path to receive mail that they found significant. Every single job has importance. No one is unimportant. Many sometimes question the importance of their labors in light of what may be happening in the world around them. But it is interesting to note that the men and women who have made the greatest contributions and discoveries were those who worked faithfully at their assigned tasks day after day. Edison didn't sit down one day and say, "I am going to discover something that will change the world." His discoveries were the result of his working routinely day after day in his laboratory. He worked routinely week after week and year after year, with thousands of failures as well as a few successes. A writer may labor year after year with one rejection slip after another until finally his work is published. The real work of the world is carried on by individuals who labor at their responsibilities day after day without recognition or praise.

How is church work carried on? Is it done by a few hired professional ministers? No, the ministry of the church is done by every single Christian finding their place to work within the routineness of the services of the church. It is done by teachers who teach, ushers who find their place of service, and individuals who work on committees, sing in choirs, or care for the babies while others worship. The work of the church is done by people who find a place of ministry in service through the routine and ordinary functions of the church. The Christian faith is carried forward by the daily commitment of the followers of Christ.

When Florence Nightingale began her nursing work in a distant land, one of the volunteer nurses who had come to assist her became frustrated by all the questions and delays they faced. Finally she said, "Stop this red tape and let me get out there and help the men who are hurting." "The strongest nurses," Florence Nightingale said, "are going to be needed at the washtubs. Come, follow me." But we don't want to be at the washtubs, do we? We want the limelight—the spectacular places to minister and serve.

God Became Incarnate through the Ordinary

Isn't it interesting that when God chose to come incarnate into the world, he did not pick the palace of a king, the seat of some great ruler, or the home of some wealthy person? God entered the world as a baby, born to parents who lived in a poverty-stricken part of the world. When Jesus taught, he drew figures from the common places of life and the ordinary experiences of people. Few have talked about commonplace, ordinary things as he did. Look at the images—farmers, seeds, birds, sheep and shepherd, flowers, yeast rising, a widow dropping in a coin, a cup of cold water. He used images drawn from ordinary, common life to describe what God's kingdom was like and what God himself was like. Too often the search for the extraordinary makes us lose awareness of what God is trying to do in our midst today.

An anonymous poet expressed that truth this way:

The moon and stars are commonplace things,
And the flower that blooms and the bird that sings,
But dark is the world and sad our lot,
If the flowers fail and the sun shone not,
And God who studies each separate soul
Out of commonplace lives, makes his beautiful home.

A Mature Approach

Out of the ordinary, the poet reminds us, God can bring something extraordinary. The Scripture lesson from 2 Kings points us to some deeper messages about life. If you and I are going to understand the greatness of the world in which we live, we have to learn how God works through the ordinary and commonplace to bring something extraordinary into our lives. If we are going to do this, like Naaman, we have to learn to be more mature. In his childishness he almost missed his miracle. When the instructions from the prophet did not meet his expectations, he was furious. He felt he was not given enough note or recognition, and in his anger he almost walked off. But his servant showed more maturity and said, "Now, wait a minute. If he had asked you to do a difficult thing, you would do that. He asked you to do a simple thing. Why not try it!"

Ah, for more maturity in life! All of us are still much like children, but the Christian pilgrimage is a call to maturity. What is maturity for the Christian? Maturity is learning to serve God without a desire for recognition. It is learning to see a task that needs to be done and then to do it without seeking attention for having done it. Maturity is being willing to serve in the most obscure place, aware that God alone may see that service and only he will declare it great. Maturity is serving without waiting for anyone else to praise us or notice what we do.

One of the temptations Jesus faced was to let his ministry be spectacular: "Climb up to the top of this pinnacle, float down, and as you float down people will see that you are God's messenger." That was the temptation of the devil. Today we find many churches and Christians yielding to the temptation to transmit religion in a spectacular way instead of letting God come into their lives to address them through the routine and ordinary dimensions of life. What a great tragedy that we miss the power and presence of God because we are not mature enough to find him in the simple places.

Recently I visited a woman who is seventy-eight years old. She told me that she was still so excited about life and wanted to continue learning new things. "I feel like a young child," she said. "There is so much I want to learn." That's maturity: not thinking we have arrived! Our minds are not closed but open. A mature Christian's mind is expansive, growing, and willing to let God speak through whatever avenue he selects.

Any Place Can Become a Shrine

Notice further that God can turn any place into a shrine. For Naaman, God took the dirty Jordan River and turned it into a miraculous shrine to him. Naaman thought that God's shrines were back in Damascus. He thought the holy places were only located there. But God used an ordinary river to produce a miracle.

Keith Miller wrote about a friend of his who decided he would visit the great religious shrines to see if he could discover something about people's experiences with God.[1] He visited Aldersgate, where Wesley's heart was strangely warmed. He went to Wittenberg and found the spot where Luther had a dramatic experience with God. He visited numerous other places, but he found nothing spectacular in any of them. He discovered that these "shrines" were just ordinary, common places. There was nothing unusual about any of them. He preached a sermon titled "Any Old Bush Will Do," based on the text describing Moses' experience on the mountainside where he was tending sheep and God appeared to him in a burning bush.

Isn't it true that God can turn any place into a shrine? While Moses was caring for sheep on the side of a mountain, suddenly a common bush began to burn, and in that experience he met God. Isaiah went into the temple to worship God as he had week after week, and suddenly he saw God high and lifted up. Jacob was fleeing from his brother and lay down to sleep at night in the wilderness, and while he was sleeping he had a dream—a vision of God. Jeremiah took a walk and saw a boiling pot and later a potter at work. Through these images, he had a vision of God's activity with the nation of Israel. Paul was traveling to Damascus, and suddenly he had a vision of Christ. All of these experiences were in ordinary places and at ordinary times. God can turn the most commonplace, ordinary things into something spectacular as he seeks to communicate with us. You may be sitting quietly by a riverbank, and God's spirit may slip into your life. God might speak to you while you are typing at your desk, standing over your workbench, laboring in your daily job, reading a book, taking care of your baby, or walking hand in hand with your spouse. God can slip into your life in the ordinary, routine places of life, and they can become a shrine. "Once the ordinary has revealed its mystery," Charles Cummings observed, "the skies may open for us."[2] Elizabeth Barrett Browning has reminded us, "Earth's crammed with heaven, and every common bush afire with God. But only he who sees, takes off his shoes."

God Can Work through the Ordinary

Go with me a step further and notice that God can work through ordinary means to bring about his healing work. In this biblical story he used water. Naaman dipped himself in the ordinary water of the Jordan River and was healed. Have you ever thought about your own body and its marvelous functions? In addition to the large and obvious parts of our bodies, there are many small parts, some even microscopic, that enable us to exist as people. The tiny optic nerve in your eyes is so small that it can hardly be seen, but if it were severed you would lose your vision. The nerves to your teeth are tiny, but no one has to be told the pain that can come from a toothache. The small membrane inside your ear enables you to hear as it responds to sound waves.

Microscopic bacteria cause the decomposition of soil as it goes busily about its daily tasks. The lowly earthworm tunnels its way through the earth to let moisture and air aid in the decomposition of the soil. A tiny sperm cell fertilizes an egg and a new life begins. The atom, which can be seen only under a microscope, is the source of the greatest energy known to mankind. From that tiny source comes spectacular power.

It is unfortunate that we often emphasize that the most worthwhile things are large and spectacular. Unfortunately, "Jumboism" is our basic philosophy of life. Does that mean the richest person in the world is the most Christian person? Is the largest nation the most Christian nation? Is the greatest person the one with the largest bank account, the largest number of oil wells, or the most spectacular record of sales? Does that mean the largest church is the most authentic church? I don't think God uses that kind of measuring rod to determine what is most significant. Through many routine, ordinary, simple things of life, God has produced some of his greatest wonders. In C. S. Lewis's classic *Screwtape Letters*, the senior devil is instructing a junior devil to find some way to communicate with people to turn them away from God. When trying to convert them, he advises, "Keep pressing home on him the ordinariness of things."[3]

When everything we do seems so ordinary, we lose our awareness of its uncommon significance. Some of the most essential happenings of life are produced as people like you and me labor daily in the ordinary, common tasks to which we are assigned or have chosen. Jesus has reminded us, "He who is faithful in a very little is faithful also in much; and he who is dishonest in a very little is dishonest also in much" (Luke 16:10). There is also a saying that "If you will do a small thing as though it were a great thing, God will enable you to do a great thing as though it were a small thing." William James, the noted Harvard professor, penned these words years ago:

> I am done with great things and big things, great organizations and big successes, and I am for those tiny, invisible, molecular forces which work from individual to individual creaking through the crannies of the world like so many soft rootlets, or like the capillary

oozing of water, but which if you give them time will rend the hardest monuments of men's pride.[4]

Christ Transforms the Ordinary

Last, notice that when Jesus Christ comes into a life, the ordinary is transformed into something extraordinary. In the sixteenth chapter of Romans is an interesting listing of names of New Testament people. It would be marvelous to know something about one of those individuals whose name is recorded there. Paul began with a reference to Phoebe, who is called a deacon. She probably carried Paul's letter from Ephesus to Rome. He then listed a couple named Prisca and Aquila. Prisca was mentioned first, probably because she came from a wealthier and more prestigious family than her husband. Paul had met them first in Corinth. Later they appeared in Ephesus, and this letter addressed them now in Rome. In his last letter, Paul mentioned that they had returned to Ephesus again. Everywhere they went they opened their home to Christians. Next Paul mentioned Rufus. Who was Rufus? Rufus was most likely the son of Simon of Cyrene, who had carried the cross of Jesus when he was crucified. Through that experience of helping our Lord bear his cross and watching him be crucified, Simon's life obviously was changed, and his own sons later became Christians.

Who are all these other people Paul listed? There are twenty-seven names—eight of them women—who ministered in the early church. Who are they? They are the ordinary people who carried on the ministry of the church. They were people like you and me, ordinary people who are unknown to us today but who ministered as servants in the cause of Jesus Christ. They carried on the responsibility of the work of Christ in the early church. Some of their names appear nowhere else in the New Testament. When Christ touched their lives, they became extraordinary individuals. When Jesus sought to build his kingdom, he did not select the great kings or outstanding military personalities or politicians or even the great religious leaders. He called his disciples from fishermen, tax collectors, ordinary and common people. Some had even been slaves. But when he touched an ordinary person, he or she was transformed into an extraordinary individual who ministered through common and ordinary ways.

When Jesus Christ saw Simon Peter and Andrew fishing by the sea, he asked them to come follow him. Their lives were changed forever. When he called James and John to come follow him and become fishers of men, their lives were never the same again. When he spoke to Nathaniel and Matthew and invited them to come follow him, their lives were made over. When he asked Zacchaeus to come down from the tree so he could have lunch with him, Zacchaeus was forever changed. When Nicodemus had his conversation with Jesus at night, Nicodemus's life took a new direction. When the woman at Samaria met Jesus Christ by the well, she could no longer live the same way. When Paul met Jesus Christ on the Damascus Road, he became a different person. No life is ever the same after Jesus Christ enters it.

Jesus Christ always makes our ordinary, routine work seem extraordinary. It may not appear extraordinary in the eyes of the world, but it is extraordinary in the eyes of God. Jesus Christ helps us see life differently. He makes us aware that all of life is crammed with God, and God is working through all of life to fulfill his purpose.

Many years ago in Chicago, Warner Sallman, the noted artist who painted a famous picture of Christ that has sold over 500 million copies, went to visit a businessman in one of the executive buildings. When he entered the office, he studied the man for a moment and said, "I think I know you from someplace. Do I not?" "No, Mr. Sallman," the business executive said. "I have never met you before. This is our first meeting." "No. I never forget a face," the artist continued. "I'll think a moment. It will come to me." After they had talked a few minutes, Mr. Sallman interrupted the businessman and said, "I remember now. You were a youth leader for the YMCA about fifteen years ago." "Oh, goodness," the businessman replied, "don't remind me of that experience. I consider that one of the most miserable failures of my life. Why, I tried to work with a group of boys, and it seemed to me that nobody ever listened. I came week after week and tried to teach them about the Christian faith, but nobody paid any attention to anything I ever said. That was the most miserable failure of anything I ever did."

"That's interesting," Mr. Sallman said. "I was one of those young men who came each week. I remember one night when you described to us what you thought Jesus Christ looked like. I was a struggling young artist then. As you talked, I took out my sketch pad and I drew a picture. Now the picture of Jesus that hangs in so many people's homes today came from the image you gave that night of what you thought Jesus Christ looked like." The businessman got up and walked around his desk. "I can't believe it. What I thought was a great failure in my life may have been the one thing that God has used far more than anything else I have ever done."

We can never judge how God may use whatever we do. As you teach a Sunday school class, sing in the choir, usher, serve on a committee, or work faithfully in your job with honesty and integrity, you serve God. How can you measure the impact this may have on other people? You can't. At times we help more than at other times. Sometimes we may fail. Nevertheless, we press forward to serve the best we can wherever we are with the gifts we have. It is required of a steward that he or she be faithful. All of life has come to us as a gift. Spend your life in whatever you do realizing that nothing God has given us is common or ordinary when it has the blessing of his presence upon it. All the ordinary things of life can become a shrine, a vehicle, through which God communicates himself to you and to others. Quit waiting for something spectacular. God is already at work through the ordinary, routine things of life. Open your eyes, open your ears, and hear him and see him.

Daniel: Principles Worth Dying For

Daniel 1:6-16

The book of Daniel has often been the happy hunting ground for crafty clairvoyants who see in it the divine plan of the ages—predictions for the coming of Jesus, the end of the world, and other matters about the "end-times." Some recall hearing about the adventures of Daniel and his friends in the lion's den in childhood Bible classes, but now that they have become adults, they have put aside such childish stories. One of the tragedies of today's church is that the message of this book has been long ignored except by those who are trying to peer into the future. These people have used Daniel, alongside the book of Revelation, to provide them with complicated charts and graphs to predict the events leading to the end of the world. Maybe the basic message of Daniel will be clearer and more meaningful if we can examine it more carefully. Go with me now on that journey.

Apocalyptic Literature

The book of Daniel has usually been classified as a type of literature called "apocalyptic," meaning "unveiling" or "revelation." Books of this type were often pseudonymous, symbolic, and esoteric. The apocalyptic imitators of Daniel were concerned primarily with the future, whereas the writer of this book was interested in disclosing the power of God for his own day and age. Norman Porteous sees Daniel as a distinctive type of writing that drew from earlier wisdom and prophetic literature as well as the Psalms to proclaim its own peculiar message.[1] The main concern of Daniel was not the future but the present. He lived during a pressing crisis, and his book was written to address that need.

The Historical Setting

In about 175 BCE, Antiochus IV seized the throne of Syria and took the title Epiphanes, which meant "the manifestation of God on earth." In the year 169 BCE, he sacked Jerusalem and robbed the temple of sacred items, including the altar. Two years later he erected a statue of the god Baal Shamem in the Jerusalem temple, and it was rededicated to Zeus of Olympus. Antiochus IV forbade the Jews to practice their religion, with the threat of death. They were forced to sacrifice to pagan gods; the Book of the Law was burned; and circumcision and other practices of their faith were forbidden. This bloody persecution was a time of personal and national crisis for the Jewish people. Judas Maccabeus took up the sword to set the people free. But his effort was short-lived, and the dark days of persecution continued.

The book of Daniel was written about 165 BCE to offer the people hope in what appeared to be a hopeless situation. To escape detection by the Syrian authorities, the writer set his story in the time of the Babylonian captivity in the sixth century BCE. He used the name Daniel as a nom de plume, a customary practice in ancient writings. There are two references to a wise man named Daniel in Ezekiel 14:14 and 28:3. There are records of a "Danel," who was wise, in the Ras Shamra texts. The writer may have based his book on these stories. The prophet Daniel and his three friends faced circumstances that resembled the struggles confronted by the Jews in the second century BCE.

A Time of Testing

The writer hoped to lift the crushed spirits of his people so they could meet their own time of testing with faith and courage. He pictured the Seleucid empire as pale compared to the splendor and might of

Nebuchadnezzar, who was "the head of gold" (Dan 2:38), superior to all the rulers who succeeded him. His image was colossal, and the torture of his fiery furnace made the idols and persecution of Antiochus seem tame. Yet God enabled Daniel and his friends to be victorious during their time of persecution. They placed their trust in God, and God sustained them. Their unflinching faith was summarized in the words of Shadrach, Meshach, and Abednego: "If there is a god who is able to save us from the blazing furnace, it is our God whom we serve, and he will save us from your power, O king; but if not, be it known to your majesty that we will neither serve your god nor worship the golden image that you have set up" (3:17-18).

The Book's Division and Dating

The book of Daniel is divided into two sections. Chapters 1–6 relate stories about Daniel and his adventures. Chapters 7–12 are composed of visions Daniel had. The book is also written in two languages: Aramaic in 2:4–7:28 and Hebrew in 1:1–2:3; 8:1–12:13. It is uncertain whether this indicates several sources for the writer or that he wrote in one of the languages (probably Aramaic) and subsequently translated part of his writing into the other language. The Hebrew literary quality of chapters 8–12 is inferior to the Aramaic used earlier. Many other suggestions have been offered for the two languages, none of which is completely satisfying.

It was indicated earlier that the book was most likely written about 165 BCE. Here is some of the internal evidence for a second-century date: the writer's vague knowledge of the details about the Babylonian and Persian period, his historical inaccuracies about that time, his precise knowledge of the Ptolemy and Seleucid periods, his use of Greek words, the development of the book of Daniel's theology, and its advanced angelology. The author was not attempting to write scientific history but to teach a moral and religious lesson about the presence of God during a time of great crisis. The main theme of the book addressed how Israel was to live in a Gentile (secular) world. The author assures his readers that with loyal obedience to God they will discover that they have the wisdom and resources to match any circumstances. Faith in God will sustain the believers even when

God seems to remain silent and hidden. God is still in control of history, and whether one lives or dies, God's power ultimately will have dominion.

The second division, concerning Daniel's visions in chapter 7, may be the central chapter in the book. It draws together the stories of Daniel when he was at one time the interpreter of dreams; now he is the dreamer or visionary. In a word, Daniel's vision relates to him that the four kingdoms, which are symbolized by four beasts, have been arrogantly blasphemous toward God and have persecuted his people. Therefore, God will destroy them and establish his own rule among nations.

The Four Beasts

The symbolism of the four beasts in 7:1-8 may be stated briefly as follows: (1) The winged lion is Babylon, and the three tusks are the three Babylonian kings known to the writer. (2) The bear is the Median kingdom (although no historical evidence can be found that the Medes conquered Babylon). (3) A panther or leopard is the Persian Empire, and the four heads and four wings represent the four Persian kings. (4) The horrible and alarming beast stands for the Greek kingdom of Alexander the Great, and his ten horns symbolize successive rulers. The small horn, without a doubt, represents Antiochus IV Epiphanes.

Major Theological Themes

There are many underlying theological emphases in the book. The following are a few:

(1) *Sovereignty of God.* The God of Israel is the Lord of history (4:22; 5:24-28).

(2) *Problem of Injustice and Suffering.* Cries go up to God for help in times of persecution and hostilities (1:1-2; 3:19-30; 8:13-14).

(3) *Affirmation of Faith.* The writer challenged the reader to a faith that will not give way to conformity (1:17-21; 3:19-30; 6:18-24; 11:40-45).

(4) *Judgment*. Daniel witnessed to the certainty of judgment as a present reality. He envisioned it as swift and terrible (4:28-37; 5:1-4; 7:19-28; 8:13-14).

(5) *History and Time*. The book indicates that the writer is primarily concerned with the crisis caused by Antiochus IV. It is an unfortunate twist to read back into the book our present-day history or to assume that the author is concerned with the unknown future (8:13-14; 8:15-19; 9:1-2).

(6) *Angels*. Here in this writing is a highly developed angelology. Daniel is the only book in the Old Testament that refers to angels by name (8:16; 10:13; 12:1).

(7) *Son of Man*. This phrase translated from the Hebrew (*ben adam*) means "a human being." There is a clear indication that the figure here is to be interpreted symbolically and used in a collective sense for Israel. Later Jesus used this as a favorite term to describe himself (7:13-14).

(8) *Ancient of Days*. Literally translated, this phrase is "advanced in days." Here is a figure of divine judgment (7:9-12).

(9) *Resurrection*. Daniel contains the clearest and highest concept of resurrection found in the Old Testament (12:1-4).

The Message for Today

The message of the book of Daniel will be missed if we do not take seriously the specific event that the writer was addressing. Knowing the particularity of the text, we are now forced to see what the message is for today. In a world filled with war, injustice, prejudice, religious persecution, pain, suffering, and evil, the cry is often heard, "Where is God?" If God is almighty, why doesn't he help the weak? Why is God so silent while injustice reigns? In a world that is largely secular, how do we live out our faith without being ridiculed? We also have to wonder whether we could withstand unjust persecution because of our faith. These are your questions and mine. These questions probe some of the same issues that the book of Daniel was addressing. The book focuses on many wonderful themes that are appropriate for today. It addresses how a faithful person strives to live in a secular and often hostile society.

Principles Worth Dying For

We should not get bogged down in the issue of whether dietary laws are important religious rules for us today. Daniel and his friends believed that there was something ritually unclean about the food the king asked them to eat. They stood by their religious principles. In a similar situation, Paul had to deal with a Christian's eating meat that had been offered to idols (1 Cor 10). Paul was concerned with the "weaker" brother. Although all things might be "lawful," he said that all things do not serve the cause of Christ. We might feel that ritual uncleanness is not an issue today. Jesus seemed to put aside such laws, saying, "There is nothing outside a man which by going into him can defile him" (Mark 7:15). Peter's vision in Acts 10:9-16 also seems to confirm this. But the particular issue in Daniel was a demonstration of loyalty to God. The young men involved stood by that principle.

Radical Faith

The story of Daniel's three friends in chapter 3 offers a fine passage on radical faith and loyalty in the face of persecution and even death. This story was meant to encourage those who were suffering under Antiochus IV. Nebuchadnezzar is depicted as a worldly authority who feels that there is no limit to his power. "Who is the god that will deliver you out of my hands?" The famous verses 17 and 18 affirm faith in God whether or not he intervenes to save their lives. The three chose death rather than worship the emperor's idol and compromise their faith. This story reminds us that God does not always spare us from suffering, pain, rejection, and persecution, but it assures us that nothing separates us from his presence (see Rom 8). Many Christian believers in Eastern Europe, South America, and Africa are confronted by the military power of a totalitarian state. To confess their faith often means economic or political sanctions, imprisonment, and sometimes death. Are Christians to conform to any and all demands of the state, even if they feel that these demands conflict with their religious convictions? The state cannot command our worship or prescribe how we should worship. Church and state are not one. We worship God alone. The fourth figure in the furnace is not a reference to Jesus. It is translated "like a son of the gods"—a divine being. Verse 28 refers to the figure as an angel. But that "figure" is a reminder that we are not left alone to face our times of testing. God is present whether we sense it or not!

The Sin of Pride

The strange story in chapter 4 offers some lessons on the sin of pride. The theme of this chapter is recorded in verse 25, where Nebuchadnezzar is told he will be disciplined until he learns the lesson that "the Most High rules the kingdom of men and gives it to whom he will." The king's condition may be described as boanthropy. This is a form of insanity (lycanthropy) in which a person imagines that he is literally a wolf. Boanthropy means a person believes they are an ox or cow. Pride, or hubris, is what Reinhold Niebuhr called man's "God almightyness." Even the king had to acknowledge that his power was from God and subordinate to it. The image of the stump that is left after the tree has been cut down (4:15) indicates the possibility of restoration.

The Feast of Belshazzar

The judgment of God is the focus of the feast of Belshazzar and the strange handwriting on the wall in chapter 5. The king had committed sacrilege by using the sacred temple vessels plundered from Jerusalem by Nebuchadnezzar. This was a coded reference by the writer to the sacrilege of Antiochus IV. He was stating that the sacrilege would bring swift and terrible punishment to the offender. A minor point here, which shows some of the historical problems alluded to earlier, deals with Belshazzar. Although he was a historical person, the son of the last Babylonian king, Nabonidus, he was never king. He did act as regent on certain occasions. This does not alter the point of the story, however. The writer was convinced of the certain judgment of God. The three fatal words, *mene*, *tekel*, and *peres*, are translated "numbered," "weighed," and "divided." These words probably stood for three kinds of coins or weights. Some have suggested that they may represent different numbers. Nebuchadnezzar was worth a *mina*; Belshazzar was valued at only half a *shekel*, and the Medes and Persians were worth half a *mina* each. You are not worth much, Daniel said. This *masal*, or parable, affirmed that God's judgment was coming upon Antiochus IV as surely as it came upon Belshazzar. The handwriting was on the wall. God was marching on!

Daniel in the Lion's Den

The story of Daniel and the lions' den (6:10-24) reveals a man who believed that the law of the land sometimes had to be superseded by a higher law. He did not break the law in ignorance when he continued to pray, but he believed that the law stood in violation to his command from God. Being a man of integrity, he would not change his normal habits of praying in order to make his praying safe. His religion was not a vague, halfhearted thing. It was vital and real to him. Later the writer of the letter to the Hebrews would include Daniel in the roll call of the heroes of Israel whose faith enabled them to stop the mouths of lions and more (Heb 11:33f.). The tale does not teach that God will externally deliver all. Daniel was delivered. But Stephen was stoned to death. Jesus was crucified. Paul was imprisoned and likely martyred. With Paul it is enough to say that nothing can separate us from God when we are in Christ Jesus (Rom 8:35-39).

Other Themes for Spiritual Nourishment

Many other passages in this book offer rich soil for spiritual growth. The passage on the resurrection (Dan 12:1-4) is one of the finest in the Old Testament. The cry of anguish, "How long, O God?" is the cry of many people (8:13-14). The concept of the "Son of Man" (7:13-14) may not have been a Messianic concept in the mind of the writer of Daniel, but he saw it as a corporate figure representing the kingdom of God; nevertheless, Jesus later seemed to utilize that figure to describe himself. Drawing on another collective image, "the Suffering Servant," Jesus linked it with the "Son of Man" to express his own awareness of the Messiah. The faithful remnant became focalized in the Messiah. The ministry of "waiting" (12:12) sometimes can be one of the most difficult experiences we must endure.

Patience is never easy to practice. But everyone has to learn that lesson, since so much of life is spent waiting. Daniel was writing to urge the persecuted Jews to wait on God. Wait with faithfulness, he urged; God's presence is assured. In asking what the book of Daniel can do for us today, Sibley Towner, former professor of Biblical Interpretation at Union Theological Seminary in Richmond, Virginia, believes that "the message that God wins, that he rescues his beloved ones from the dust of the earth, and that all faithfulness is a foretaste of that victory, empowers the believer to take part in the effort to build a world which looks more and more like the Kingdom in advance." This essential message, he asserts, "can undergird an interim ethic which is expectant, hopeful and vigorous."[2]

Down through the centuries and even into our present day, Jews have suffered persecution. One of the worst periods came during the Second World War from the Nazi atrocities at concentration prisons like Auschwitz and others. Viktor Frankl in *Man's Search for Meaning* and Elie Wiesel in *Night* describe their awful experiences in such places. Frankl declared that Nietzsche's words "He who has a why to live for can bear almost any how" gave him assurance during those times of suffering.[3] Wiesel confessed "to having rebelled against the Lord, but I have never repudiated Him."[4] Waiting for God's assurance during such suffering is never easy.

Likewise, Christians have experienced persecution through the years as well. Jesus warned his followers of this fact in one of the Beatitudes: "Blessed are those who are persecuted for righteousness' sake, for theirs is the kingdom of God" (Matt 5:10). Christians indeed have suffered rejection, ridicule, torture, imprisonment, floggings, trials, and even death as they followed the Christ-like way. Many of Paul's letters, as well as Hebrews and other epistles, sought to offer encouragement and hope to Christians who were persecuted for their faith. In some countries today, Christians still suffer under hostile governments, and in our own country, some experience discrimination, ostracism, and derision because of their faith. In the face of suffering and rejection, Paul reminds us that nothing ultimately separates us from God when we are "in Christ Jesus, our Lord" (Rom 8:39). Let us live out our faith with that assurance.

Notes

Chapter 1

1. *As You Like It*, Act 2, sc. 1.

2. Phyllis Trible, *God and the Rhetoric of Sexuality* (Philadelphia: Fortress Press, 1978), 102ff.

3. Claus Westermann, *Genesis: A Practical Commentary* (Grand Rapids: Eerdmans Publishing Co., 1987), 22.

4. Dietrich Bonhoeffer, *Creation and Fall: A Theological Interpretation of Genesis 1–3* (London: SCM Press, 1962), 77.

5. Walter Brueggemann, *Genesis: A Bible Commentary for Teaching and Preaching* (Atlanta: John Knox Press, 1982), 41–43.

6. Emil Brunner, *Dogmatics*, The Christian Doctrine of Creation and Redemption, vol. 2, trans. Olive Wyon (London: Lutterworth Press, 1955), 98.

7. Terence E. Fretheim, *The Book of Genesis*, The New Interpreter's Bible, vol. 1 (Nashville: Abingdon Press, 1994), 368.

8. Walter Russell Bowie, *The Book of Genesis*, The Interpreter's Bible, vol. 1 (Nashville: Abingdon-Cokesbury Press, 1952), 503.

9. Brunner, *Dogmatics*, 100.

10. Daniel G. Bagby, *Seeing through Our Tears: Why We Cry, How We Heal* (Minneapolis: Augsburg Fortress, 1999), 51.

11. William Powell Tuck, *Facing Grief and Death: Living with Dying* (Cleveland, TN: Parson's Porch, 2013), and *A Positive Word for Christian Lamenting: Funeral Homilies* (Gonzalez, FL: Energion Publications, 2016).

Chapter 2

1. William C. Archie, "Where Have All the Heroes Gone?" unpublished address delivered at King College, Bristol, TN, November 18, 1969.

2. Elie Wiesel, *Messengers of God* (New York: Random House, 1976), 62.

3. H. Wheeler Robinson, *The Religious Ideas of the Old Testament* (New York: Charles Scribner's Sons, 1921), 87.

4. Myron C. Madden, *Blessing: Giving the Gift of Power* (Nashville: Broadman Press, 1988), 25.

5. G. Henton Davies, *Genesis*, The Broadman Bible Commentary (Nashville: Broadman Press, 1969), 198.

6. Ralph H. Elliott, *The Message of Genesis* (St. Louis: The Bethany Press, 1961), 144.

7. Gerhard Von Rad, *Genesis* (Philadelphia: The Westminster Press, 1971), 239.

8. Walter Brueggemann, *Genesis* (Atlanta: John Knox Press, 1982), 190–91.

9. Wiesel, *Messengers of God*, 84.

Chapter 4

1. George Orwell, *Nineteen Eighty-Four* (New York: New American Library, 1961), 211.

2. Keith Miller, *Habitation of Dragons* (Waco, TX: Word Books, 1970), 183–84.

Chapter 5

1. Carlyle Marney, *Beggars in Velvet* (New York: Abingdon Press, 1950), 25.

2. Boris Pasternak, *Doctor Zhivago* (New York: Pantheon Books, Inc., 1958), 355.

Chapter 6

1. Literally *yam suph* is better translated "sea of reeds" from the Hebrew words. A wrong translation of the LXX made its way into the English version because the translators knew Greek better than they did Hebrew.

2. Martin Buber, *Moses* (Atlanta Highlands, NJ: Humanities Press International, 1988), 17.

Chapter 7

1. R. F. Johnson, "Caleb," *The Interpreter's Dictionary of the Bible*, ed. George A. Buttrick (Nashville: Abingdon Press, 1962), 483.

Chapter 8

1. Alexander Maclaren, *The Life of David* (Grand Rapids: Baker Book House, 1955), 4.

2. George Matheson, *The Representative Men of the Bible* (New York: A. C. Armstrong and Son, 1902), 276.

3. Frederick Buechner, *Peculiar Treasures* (San Francisco: Harper & Row, 1979), 41.

4. With appreciation to Frank Eakin, Old Testament scholar at the University of Richmond, for this insight.

Chapter 9

1. Arthur John Gossip, *The Hero in Thy Soul* (Edinburgh: T. & T. Clark, 1926), 111.

Chapter 10

1. Lloyd John Ogilvie, *A Life Full of Surprises* (Nashville: Abingdon Press, 1969), 4.

2. Paul Scherer, *The Word God Sent* (New York: Harper and Row, 1965), 242–43.

Chapter 11

1. Scholars divide the book of Isaiah into three sections by three different authors: chapters 1–39, Isaiah of the eighth century BCE in Judah; chapters 40–55, anonymous Deutero-Isaiah of the sixth century Babylonian exile; and chapters 56–66, anonymous Trito-Isaiah of the sixth or fifth century, back in Judah.

Chapter 12

1. Phyllis Trible, *God and the Rhetoric of Sexuality* (Philadelphia: Fortress Press, 1978), 173.

2. Katharine Doob Sakenfeld, *Ruth*, Interpretation, A Bible Commentary for Teaching and Preaching (Louisville, KY: John Knox Press, 1999), 15.

3. Eric C. Rust, *The Book of Ruth*, The Layman's Bible Commentary, vol. 6 (Richmond, VA: John Knox Press, 1961), 76.

4. Trible, *God and the Rhetoric of Sexuality*, 173.

5. Sakenfeld, *Ruth*, 88.

Chapter 13

1. Lewis Bayles Paton, *The Book of Esther*, International Critical Commentary (Edinburgh: T. & T. Clark, 1908), 97.

2. J. G. McConville, *Ezra, Nehemiah, and Esther* (Philadelphia: The Westminster Press, 1985), 153.

3. Sidnie White Crawford, *The Book of Easter*, The New Interpreter's Bible, vol. 3 (Nashville: Abingdon Press, 1999), 873.

4. Desmond Tutu, *The Rainbow People of God* (New York: Doubleday, 1994), 64.

Chapter 14

1. Walter Brueggemann, *1 Kings* (Atlanta: John Knox Press, 1982), 88.

2. Sherwood Eddy, *Eighty Adventurous Years* (New York: Harper & Brothers, 1955), 27.

Chapter 15

1. Keith Miller, *Habitation of Dragons* (Waco, TX: Word Books, 1970), 62–63.

2. Charles Cummings, *The Mystery of the Ordinary* (San Francisco: Harper & Row, 1982), x.

3. C. S. Lewis, *The Screwtape Letters* (London: Fontana Books, 1956), 14.

4. *From the Letters of William James* 14/8 (September 2003).

Chapter 16

1. Norman W. Porteous, *Daniel: A Commentary*, The Old Testament Library (Philadelphia: Westminster Press, 1965), 16.

2. W. Sibley Towner, *Daniel*, Interpretation: A Bible Commentary for Teaching and Preaching (Atlanta: John Knox Press, 1984), 180.

3. Viktor Frankl, *Man's Search for Meaning* (New York: Washington Square Press, Inc., 1963), 121.

4. Elie Wiesel, *Open Heart* (New York: Schocken Books, 2012), 68.

Made in the USA
Columbia, SC
19 June 2022